SYMMETRY ART

A SYMMETRICAL DRAWING ACTIVITY BOOK FOR Kids

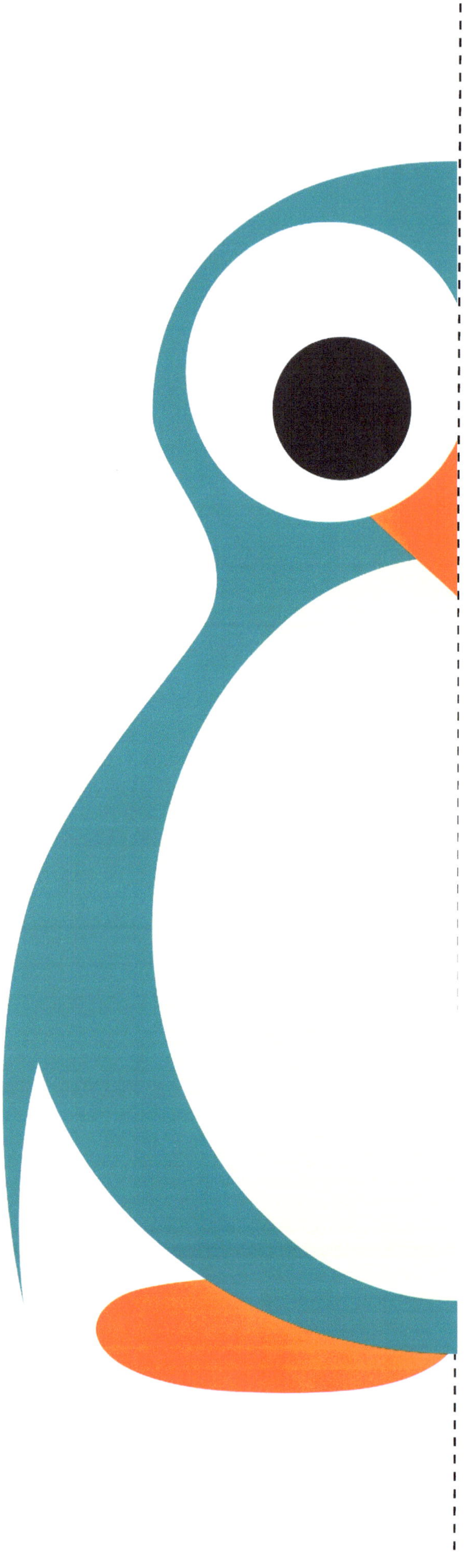

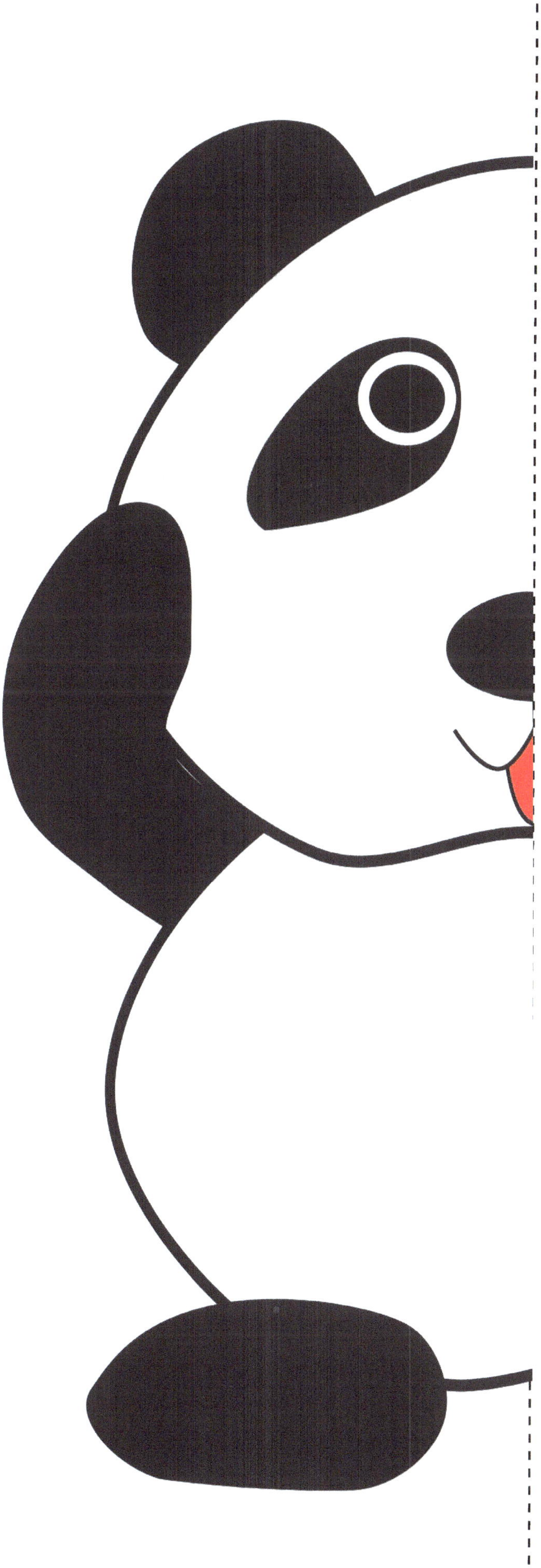

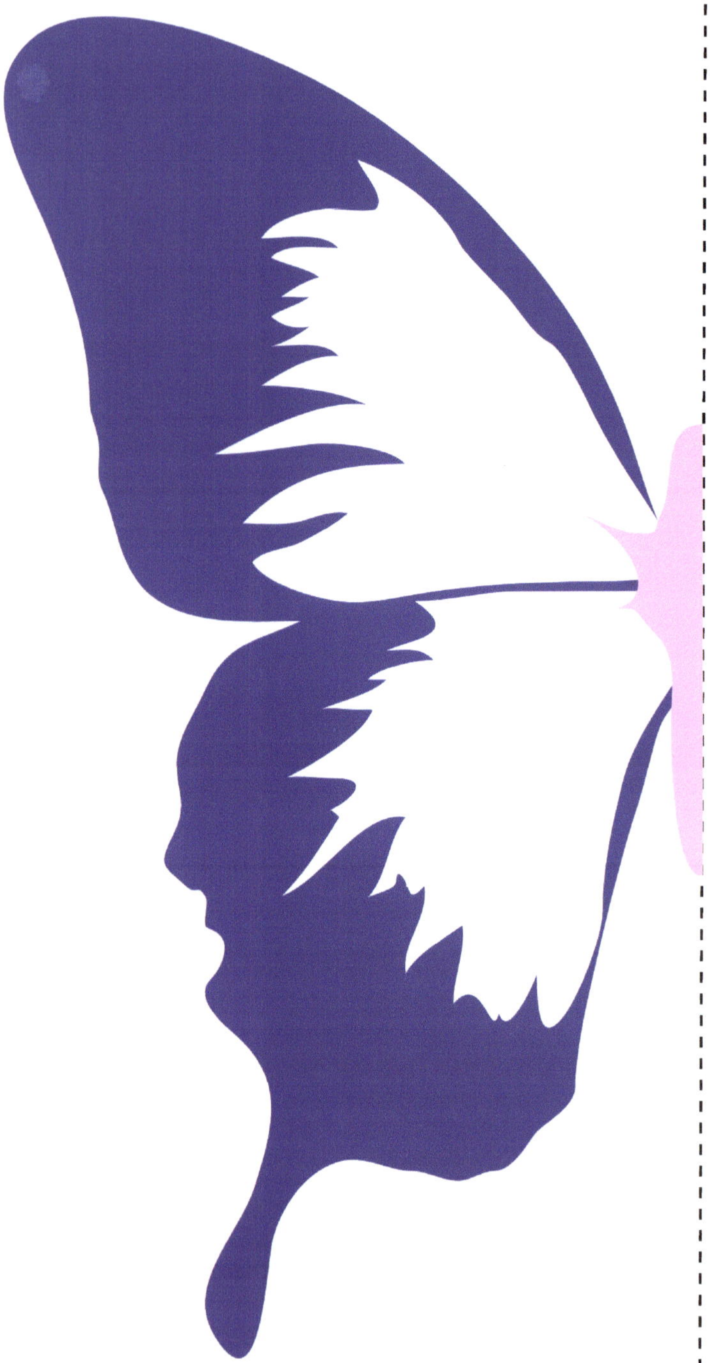

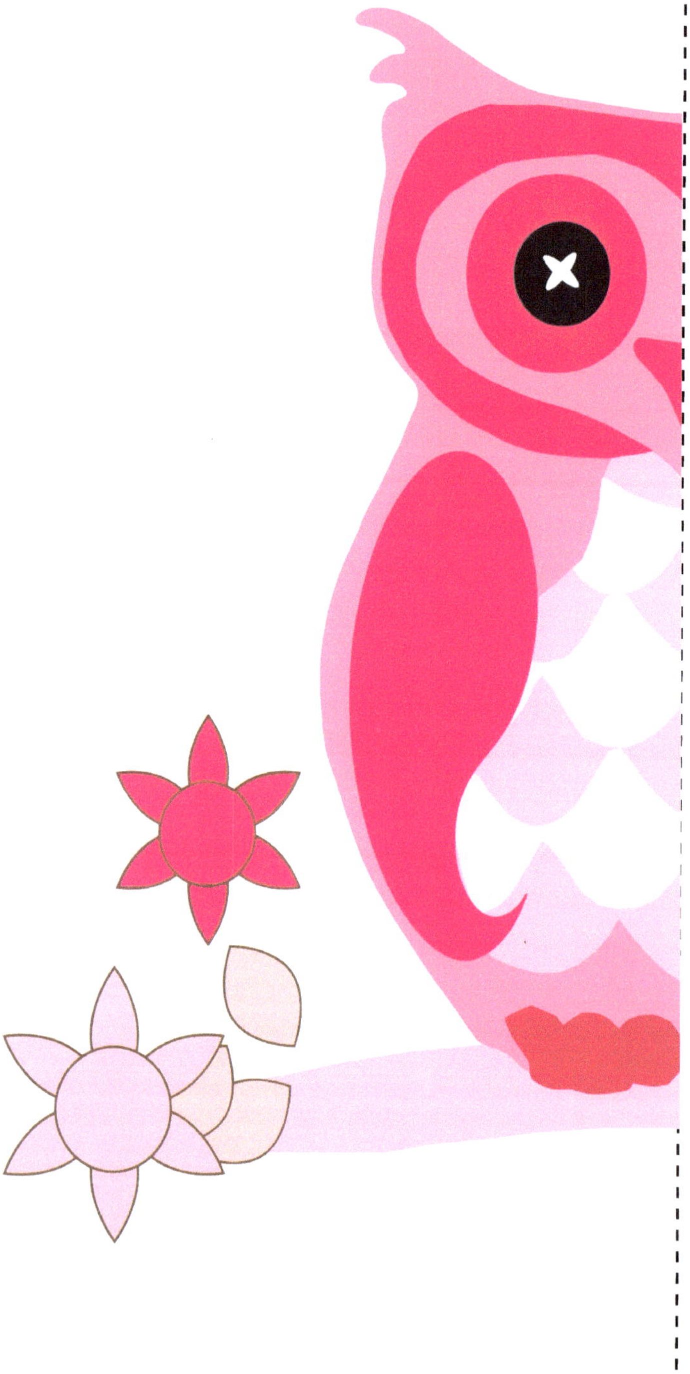

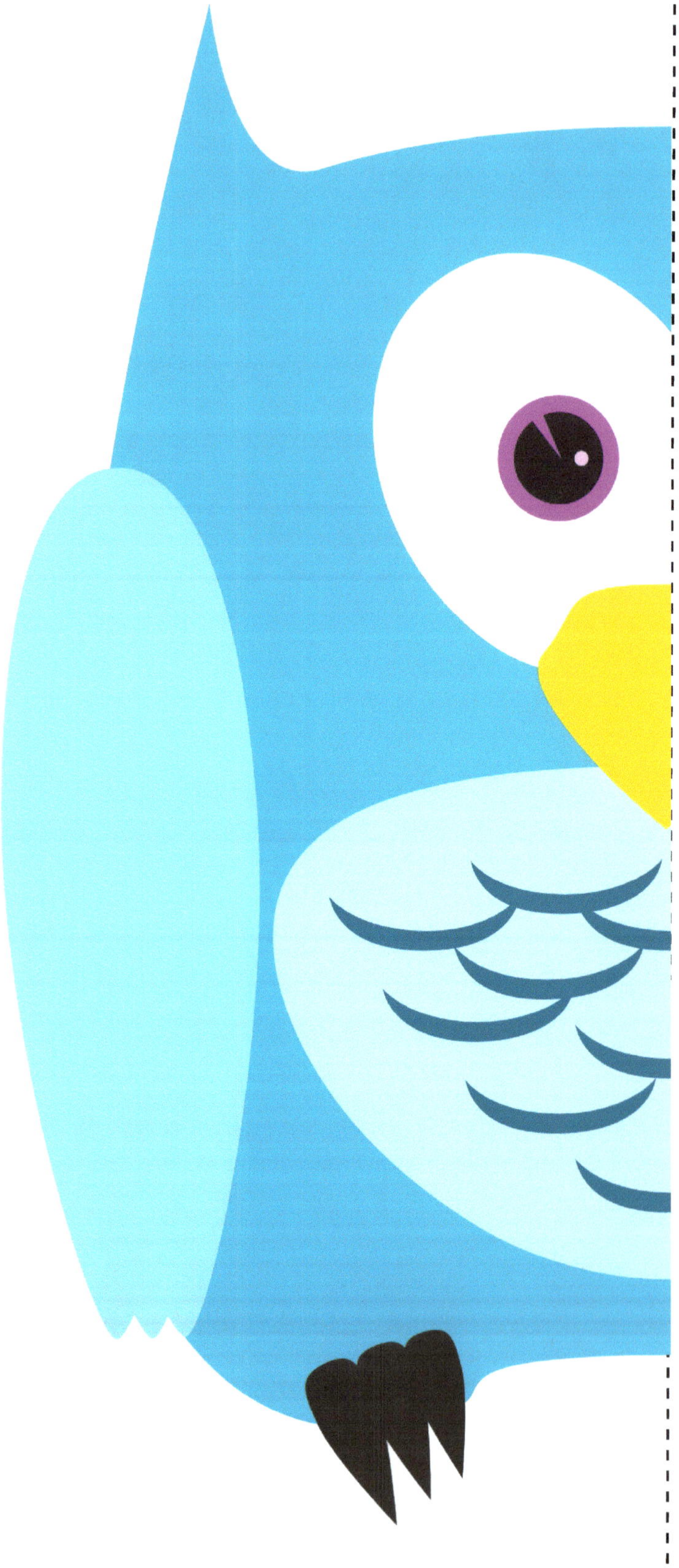

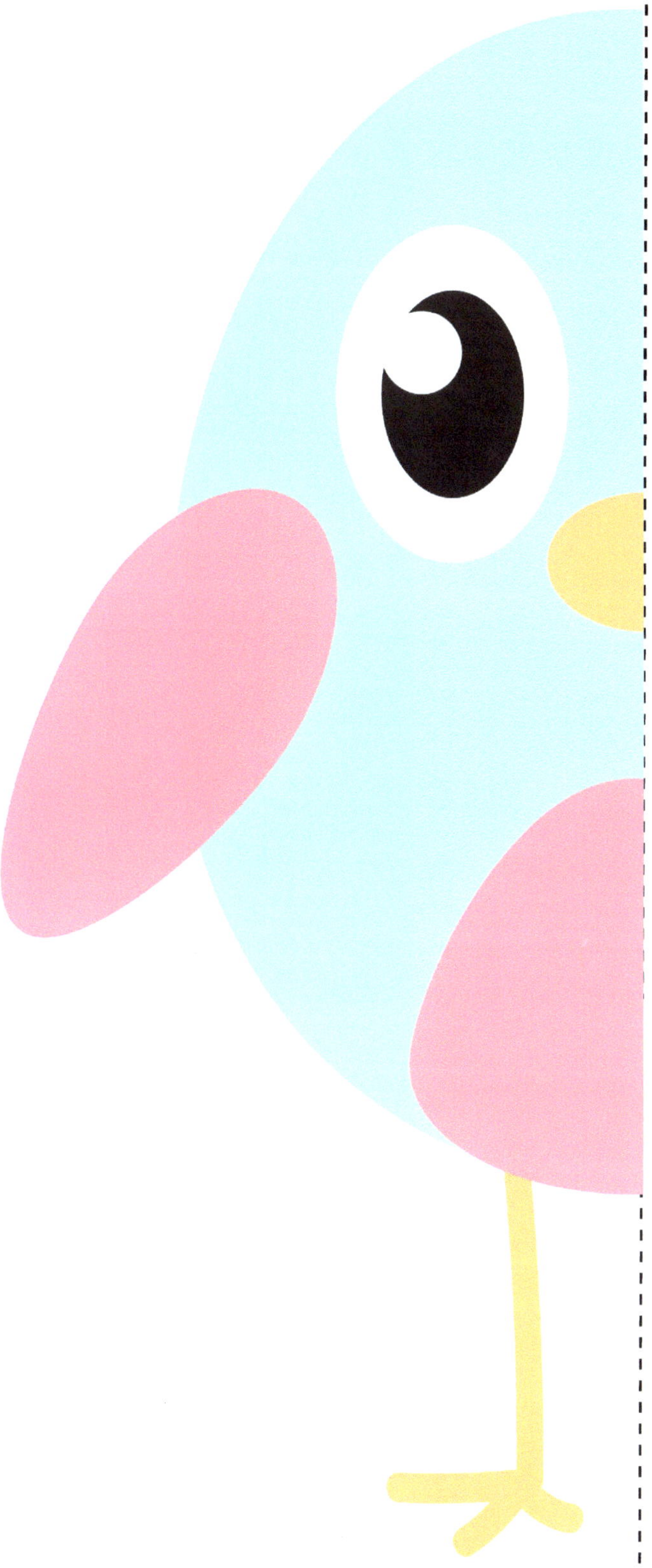

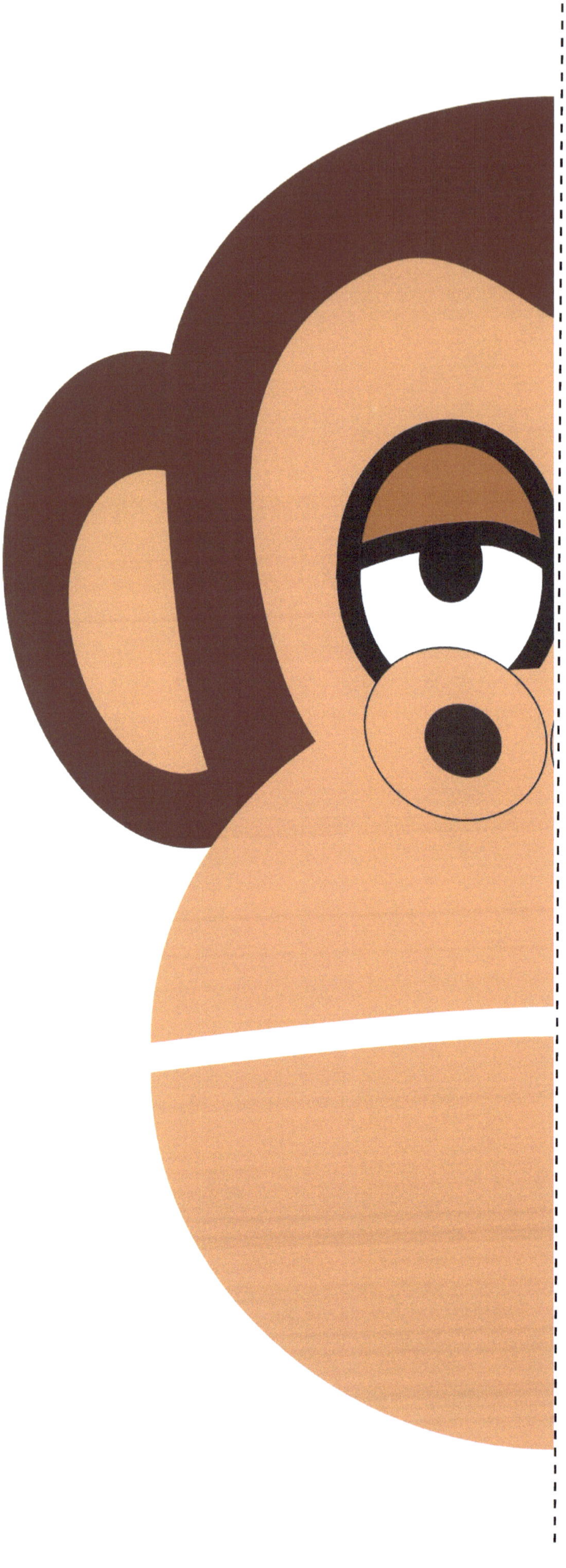

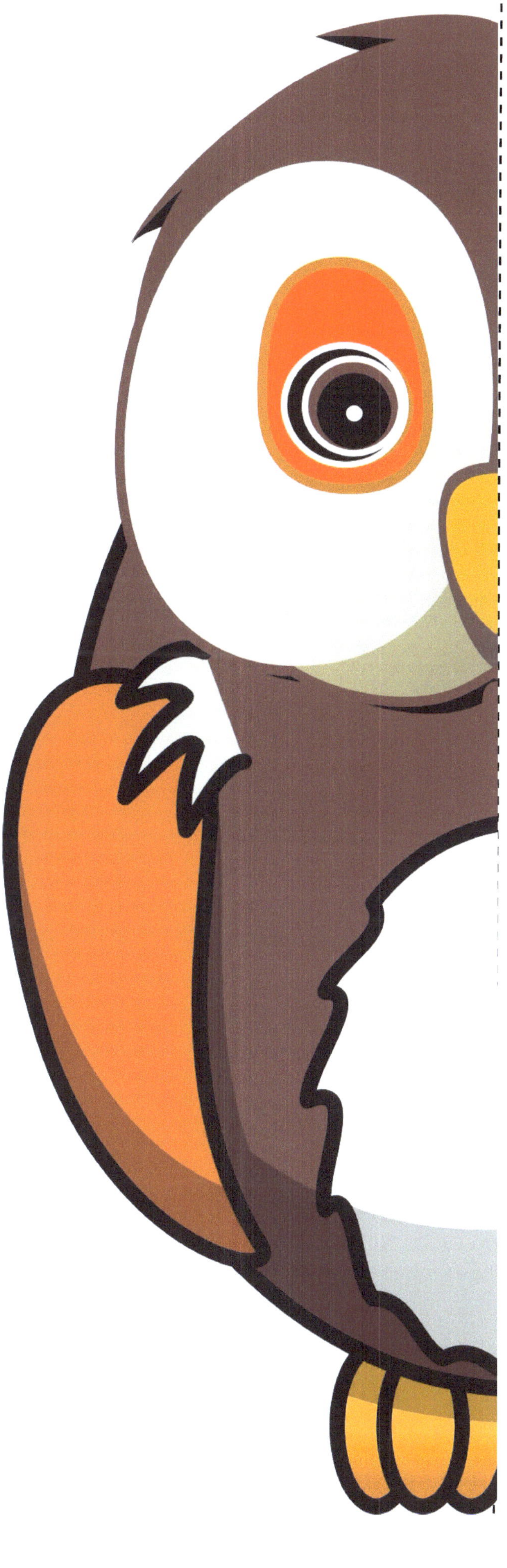

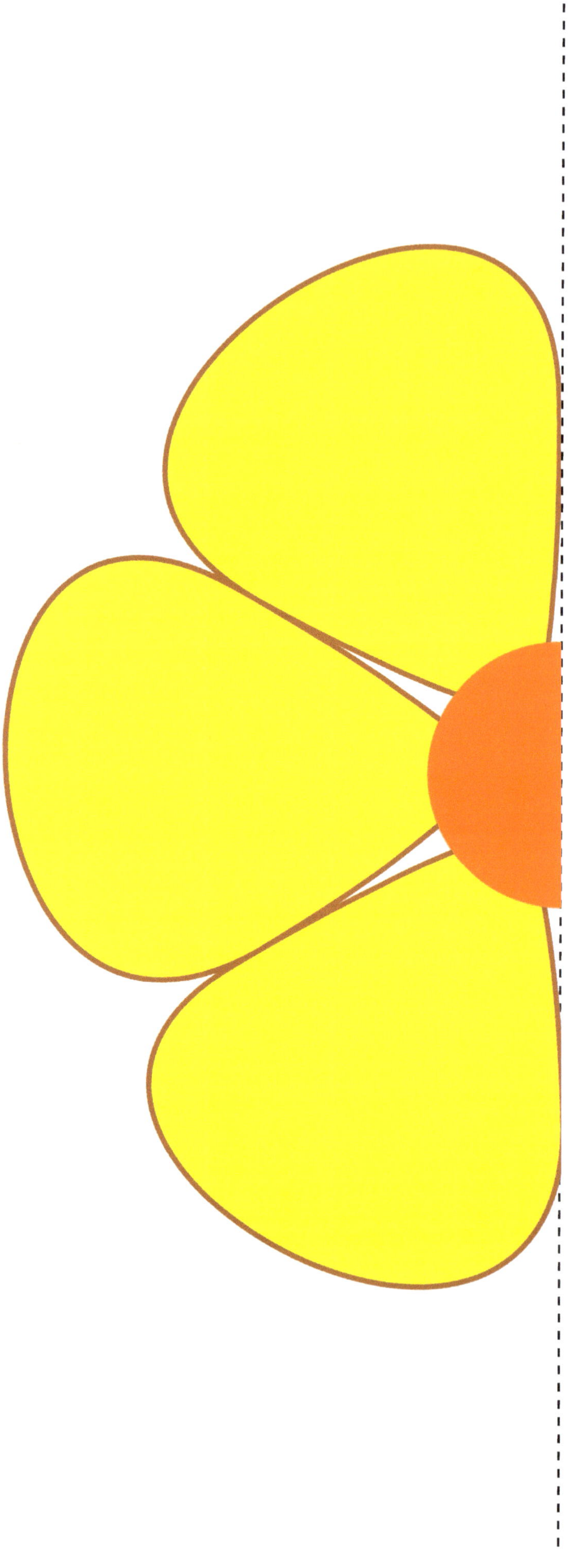

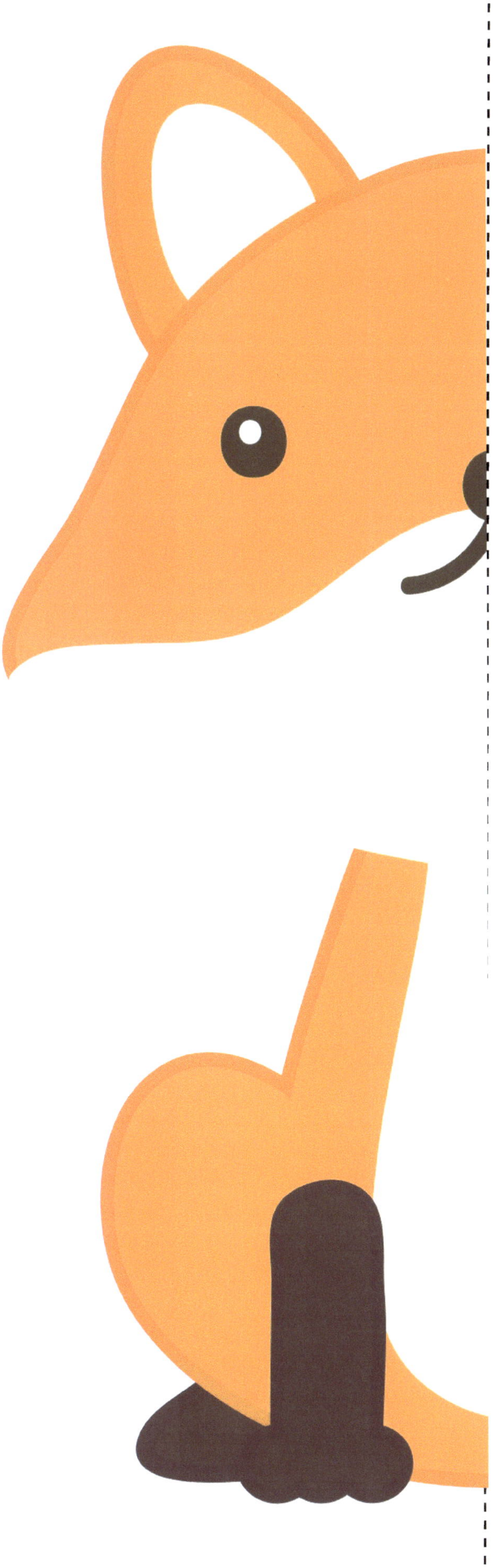

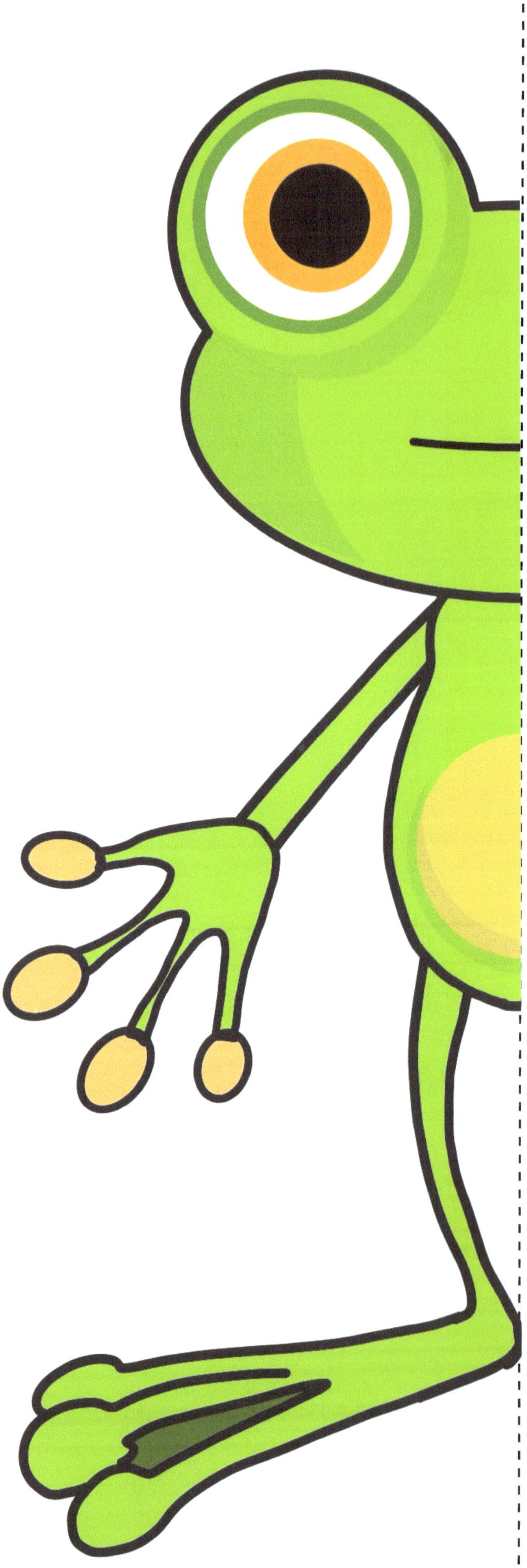

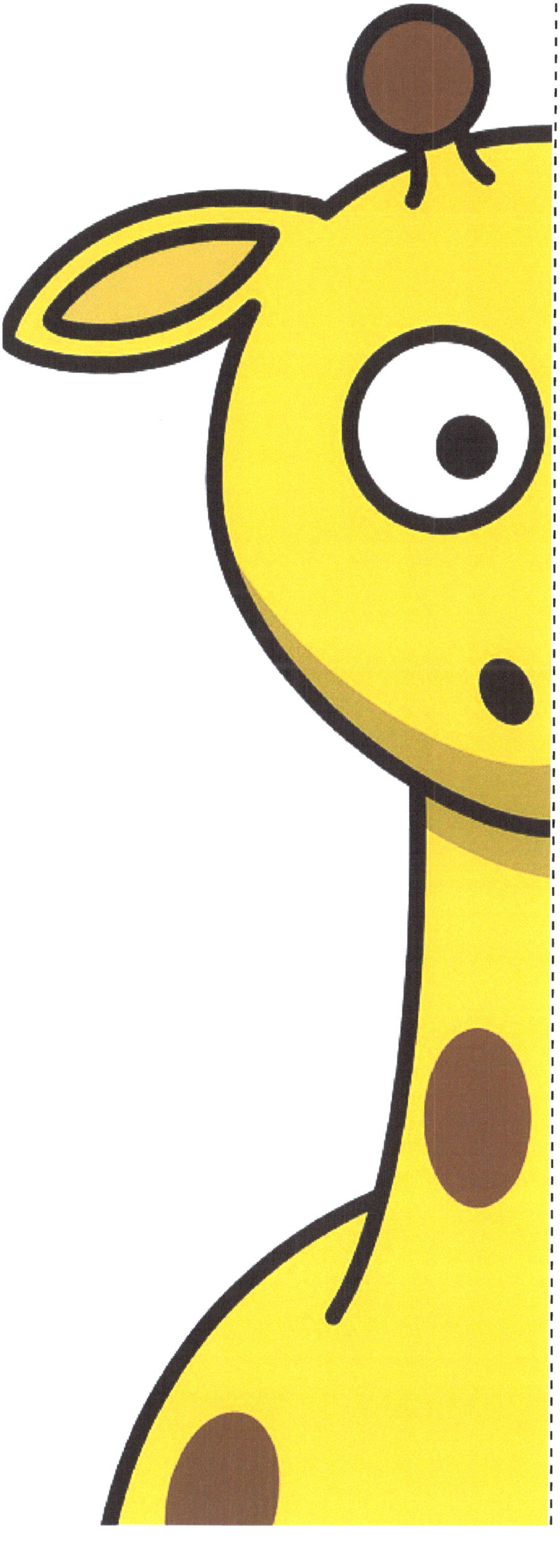

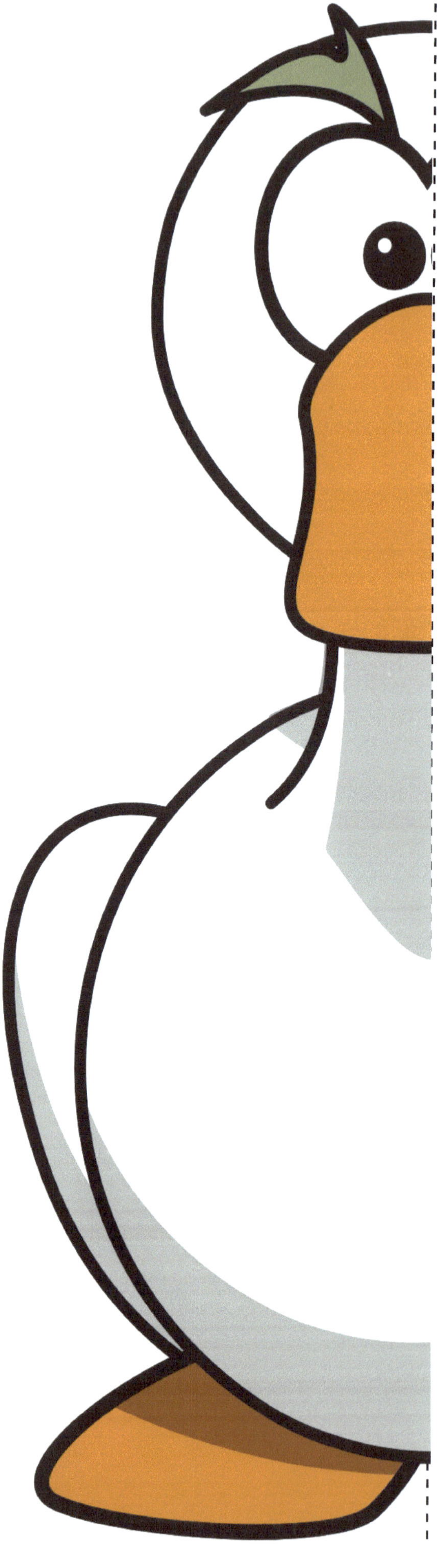

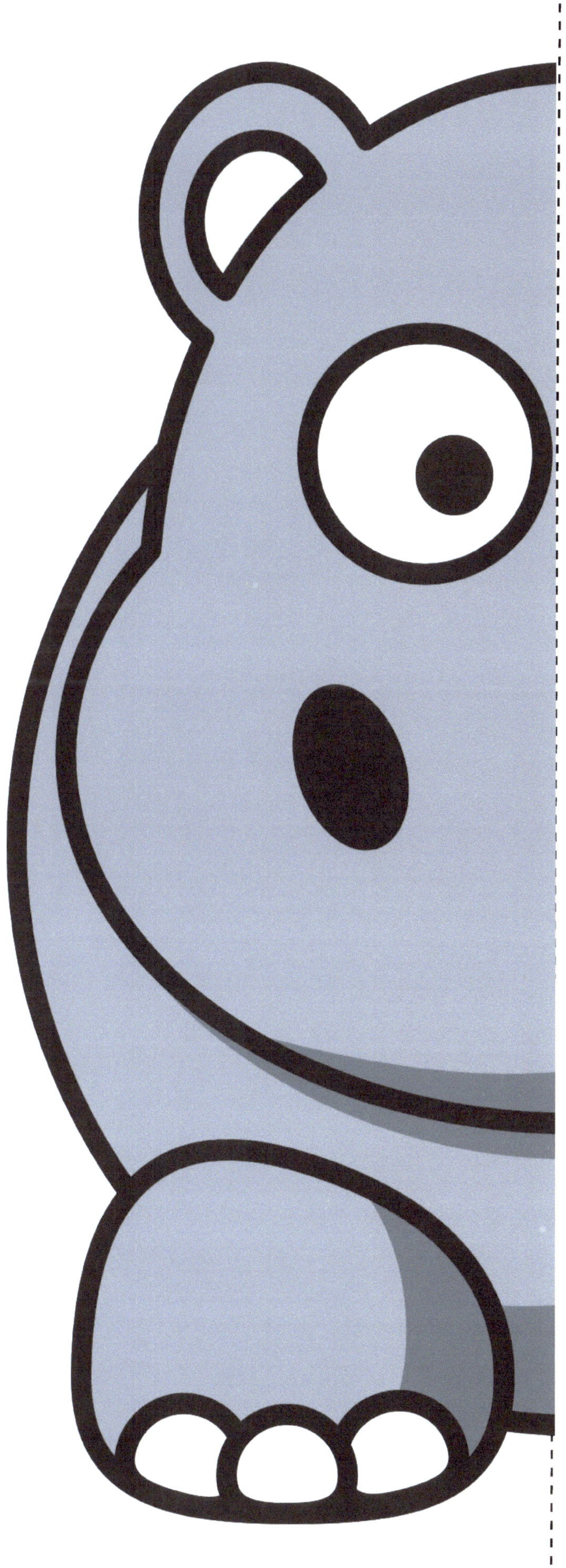

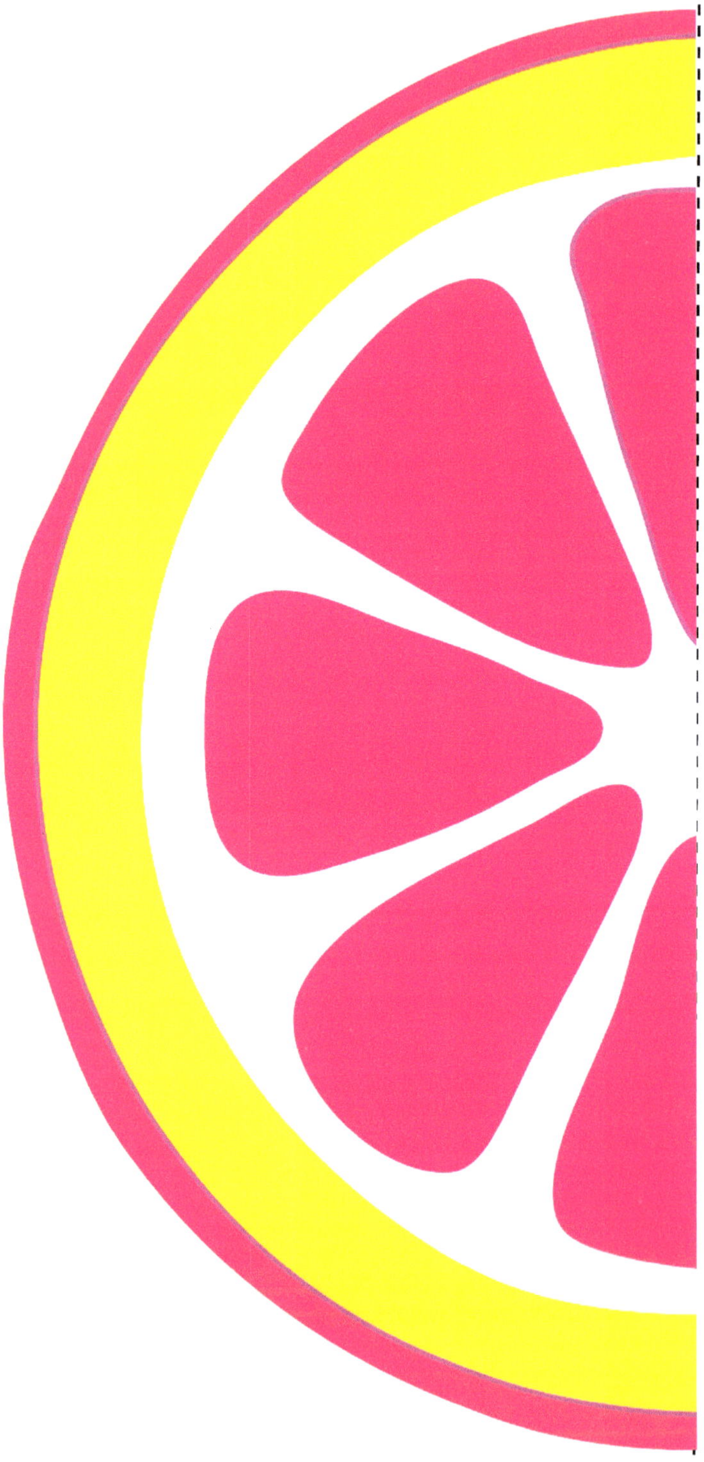

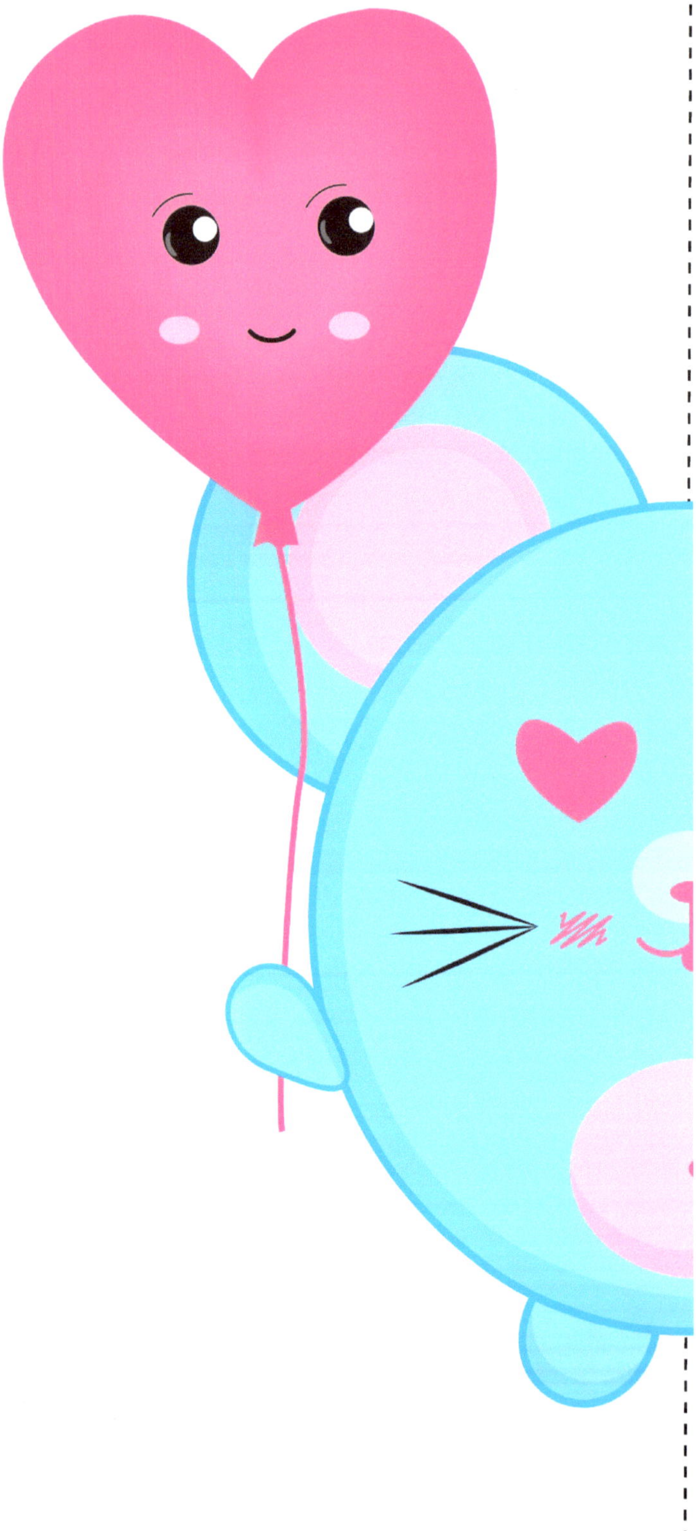

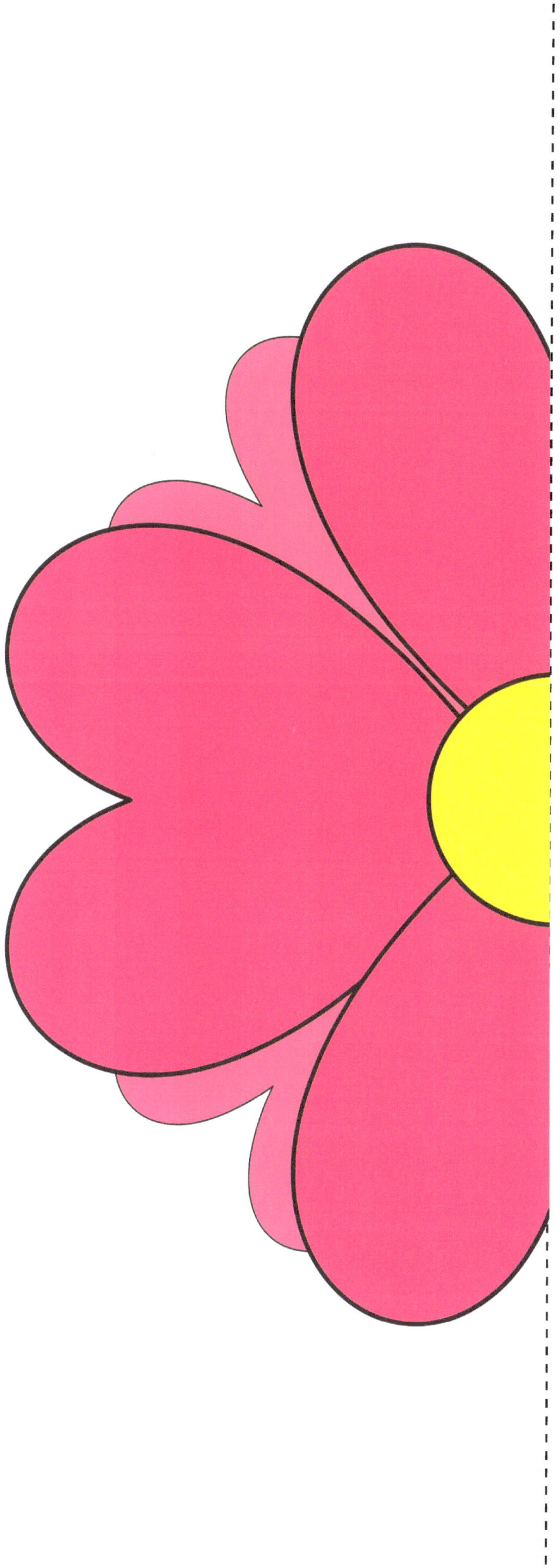

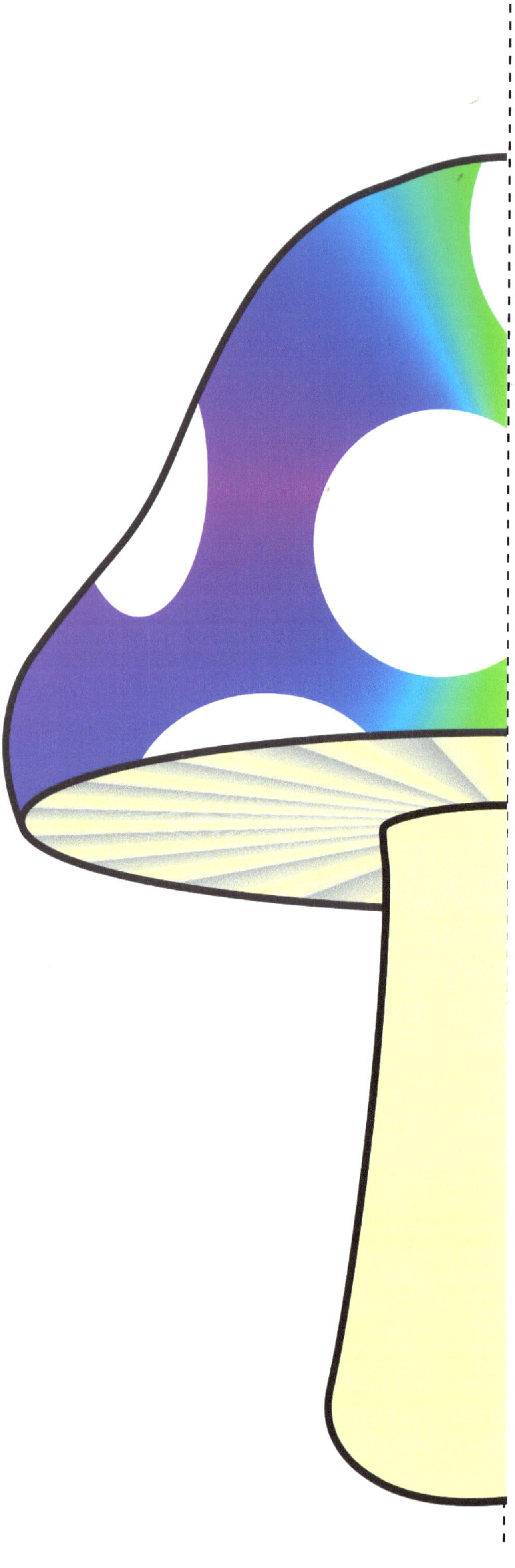

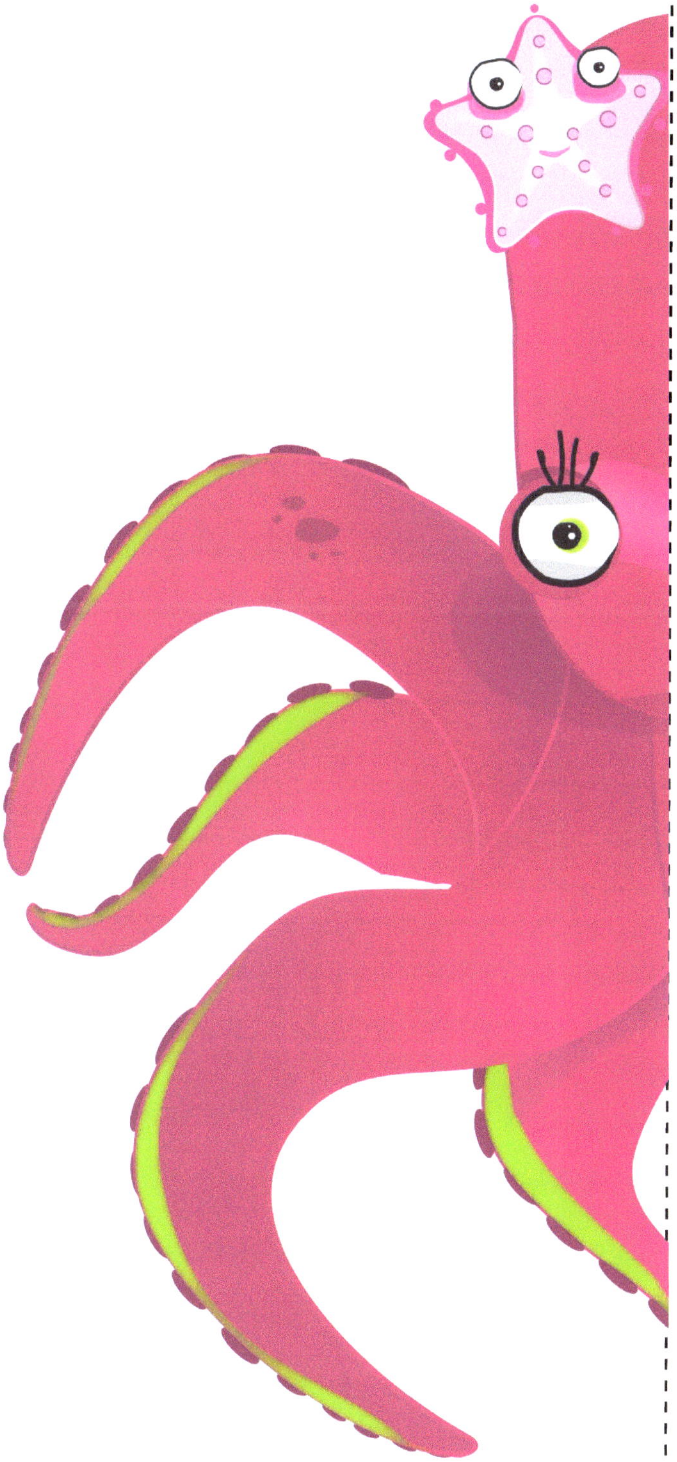

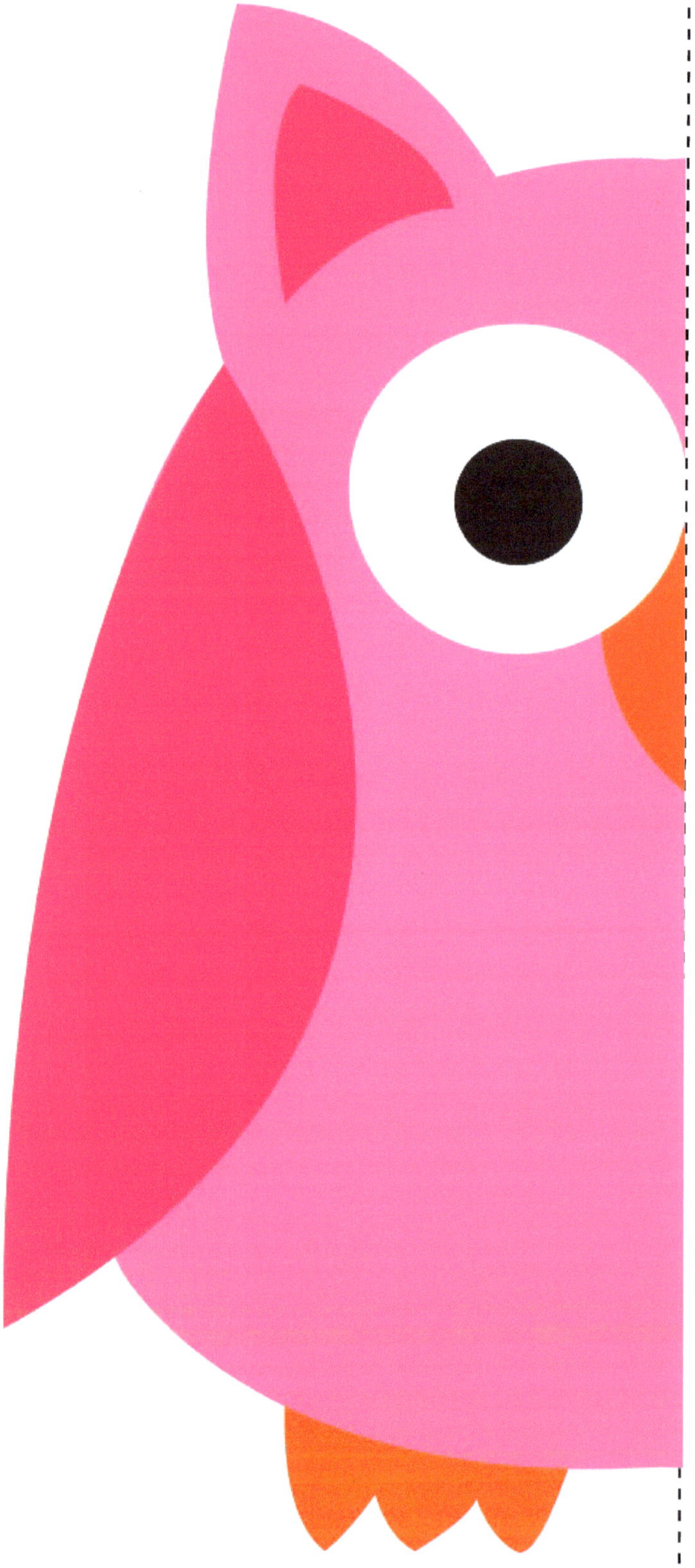

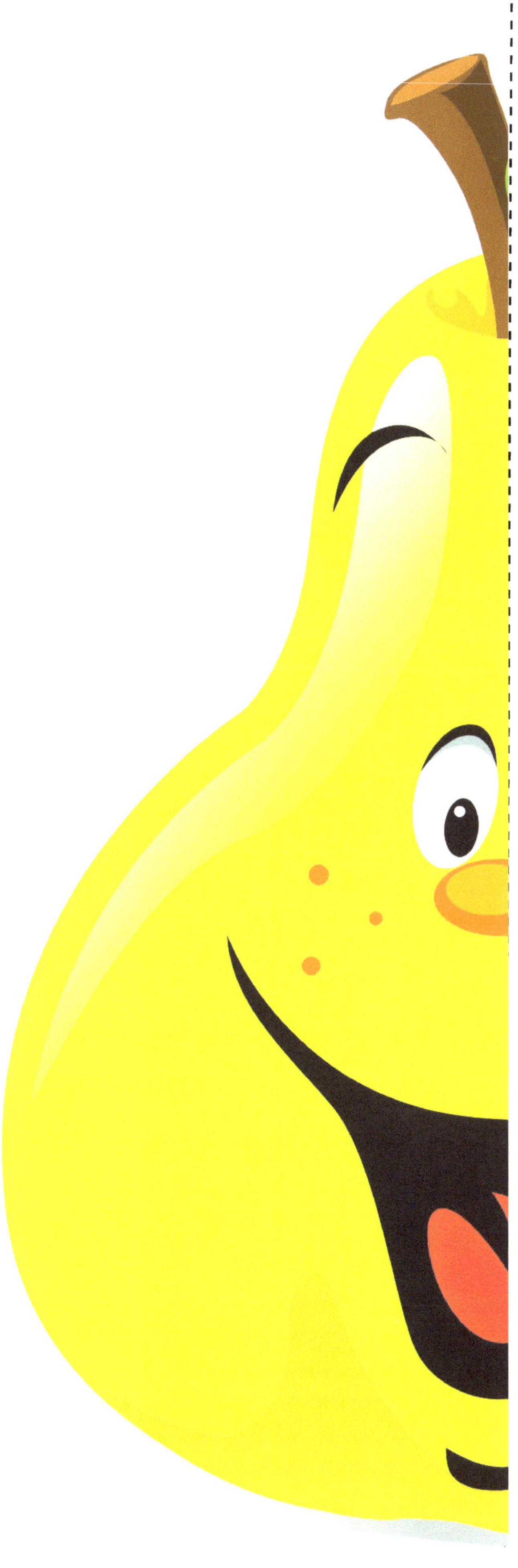

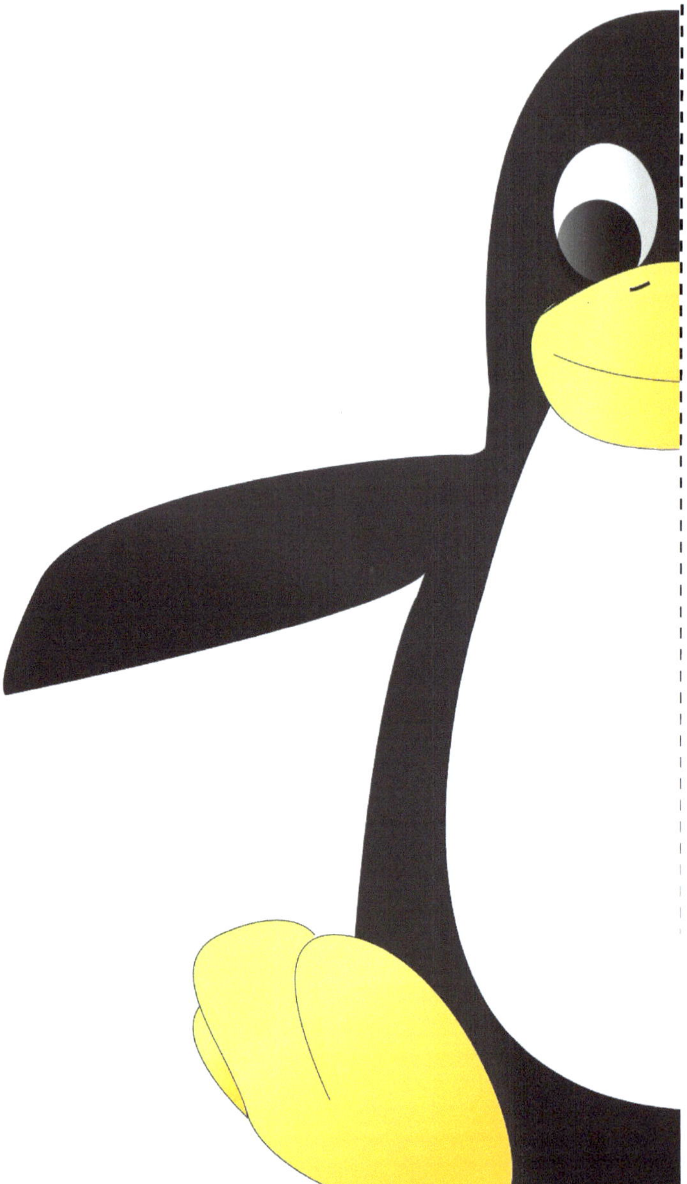

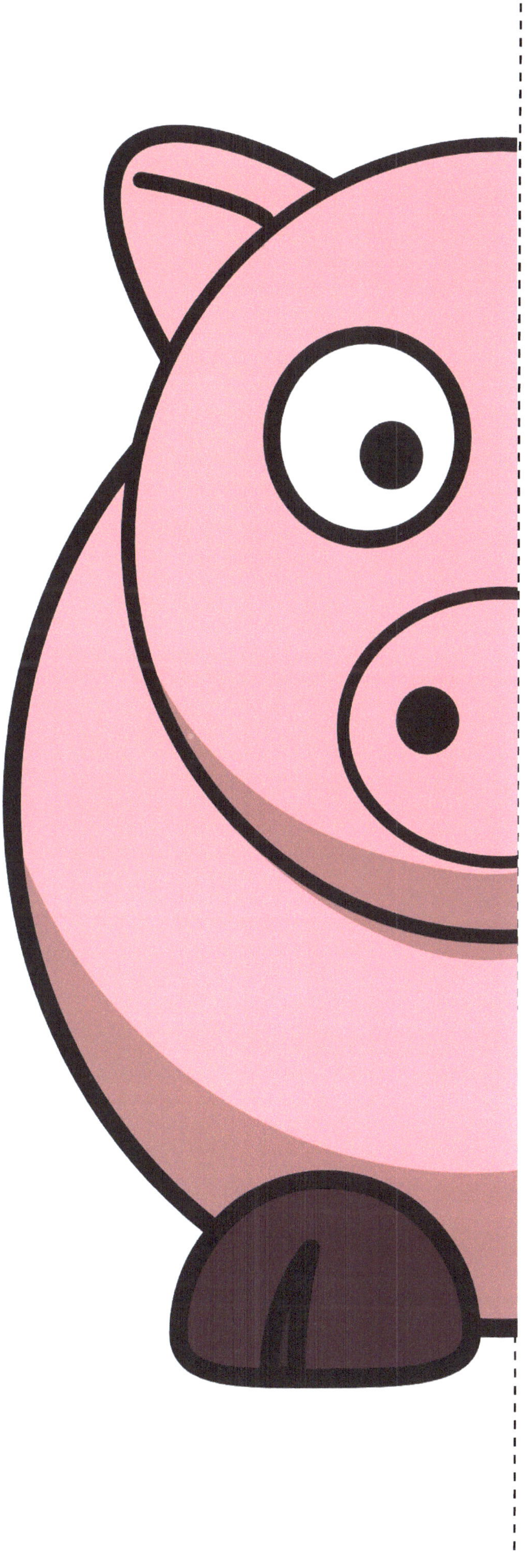

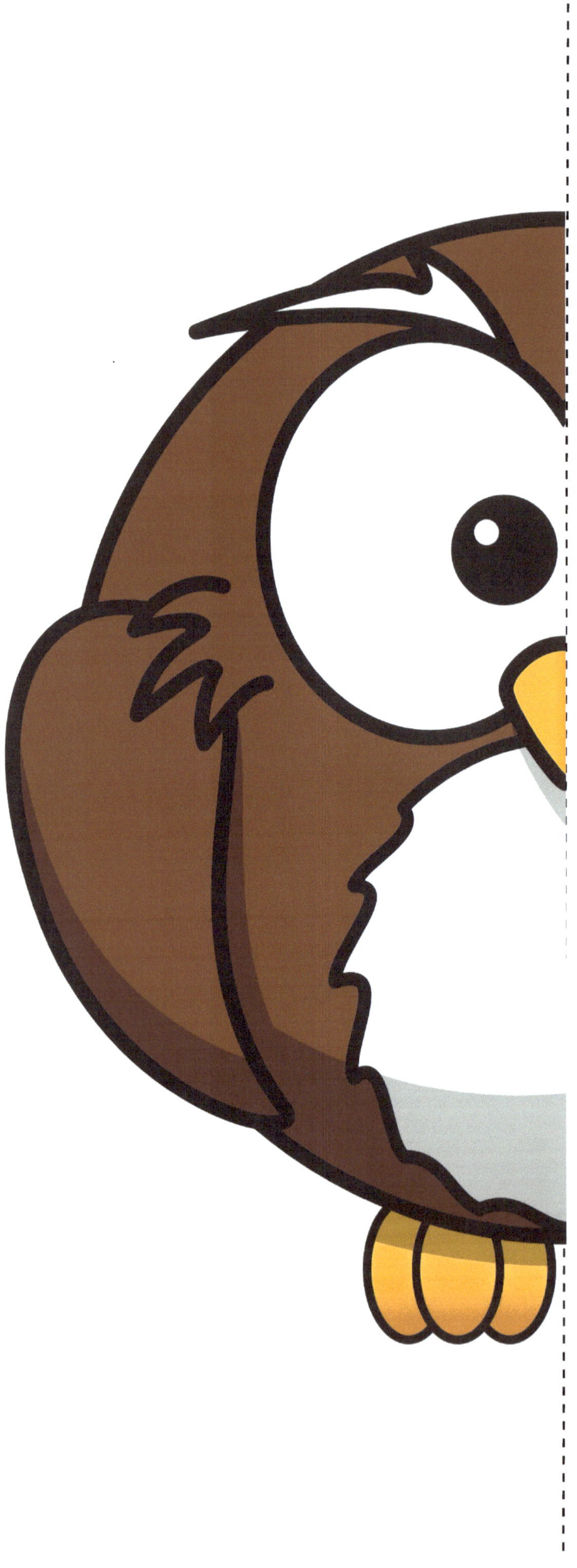

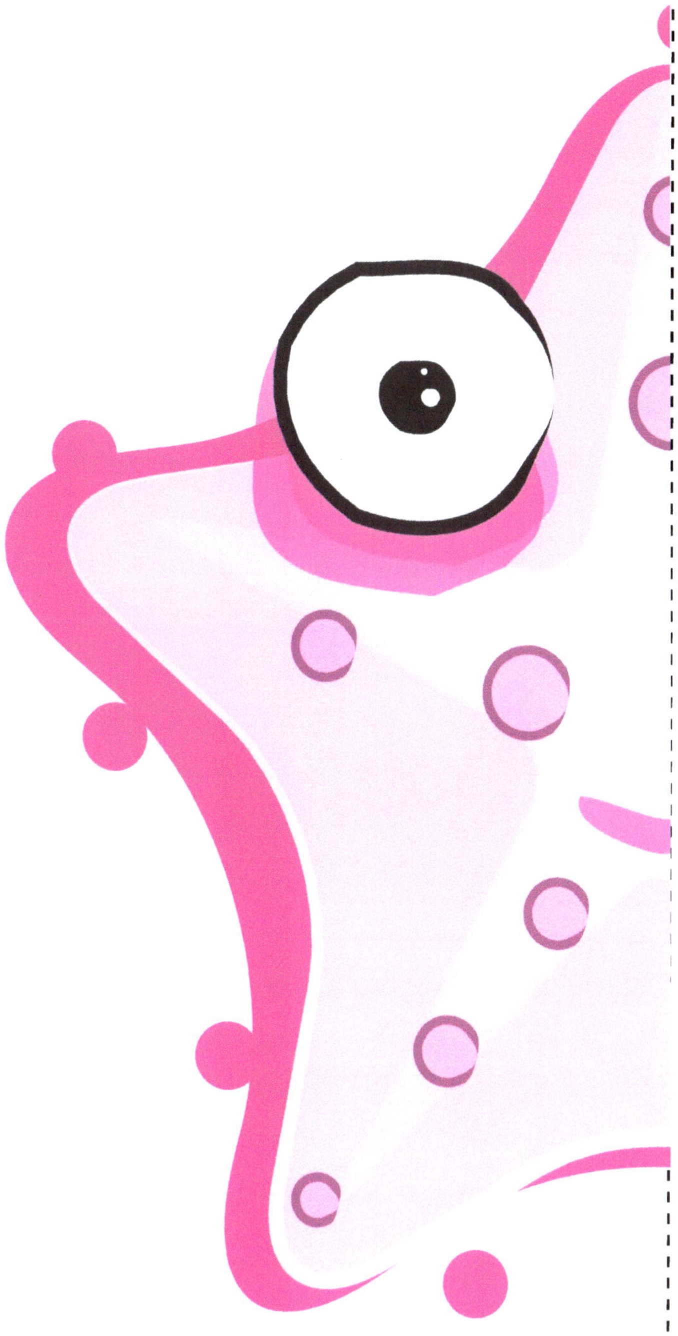

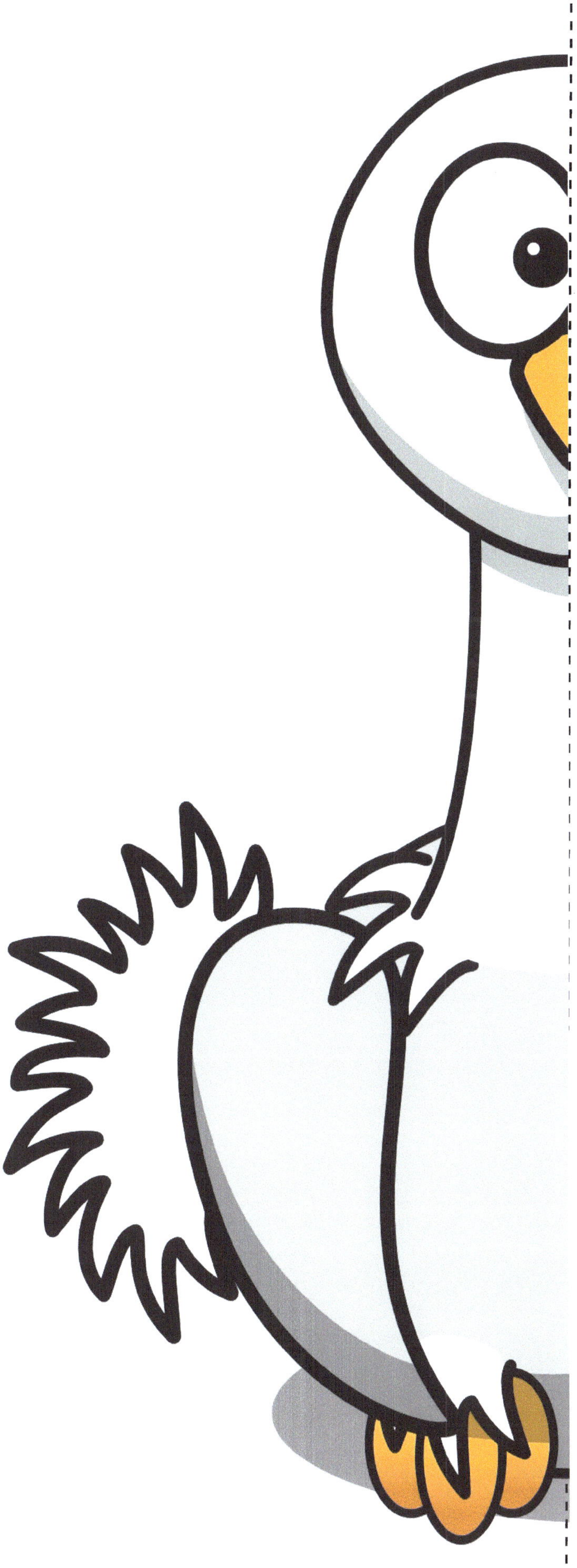

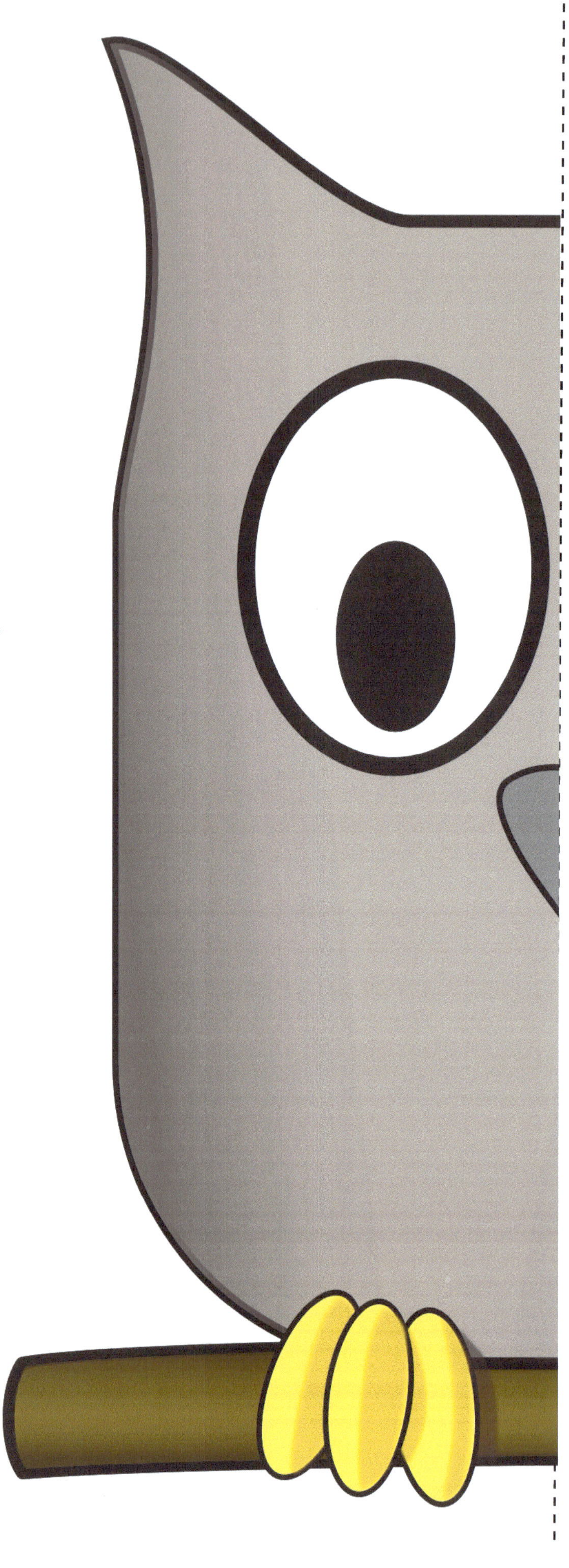

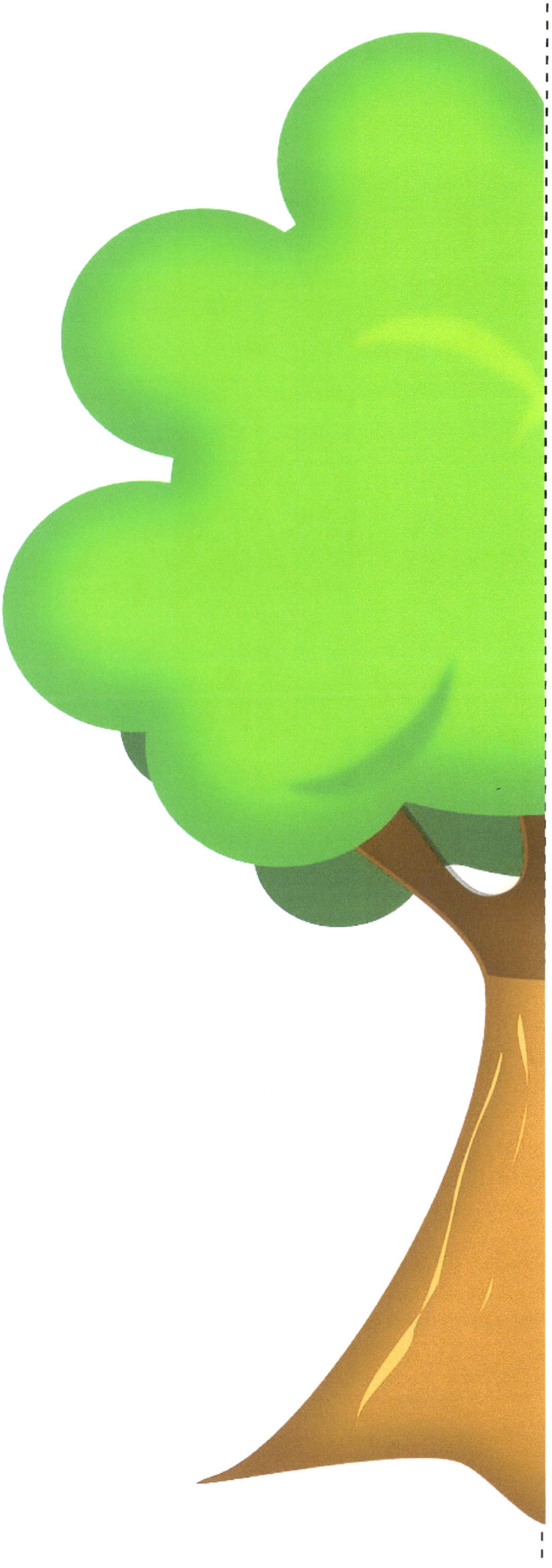

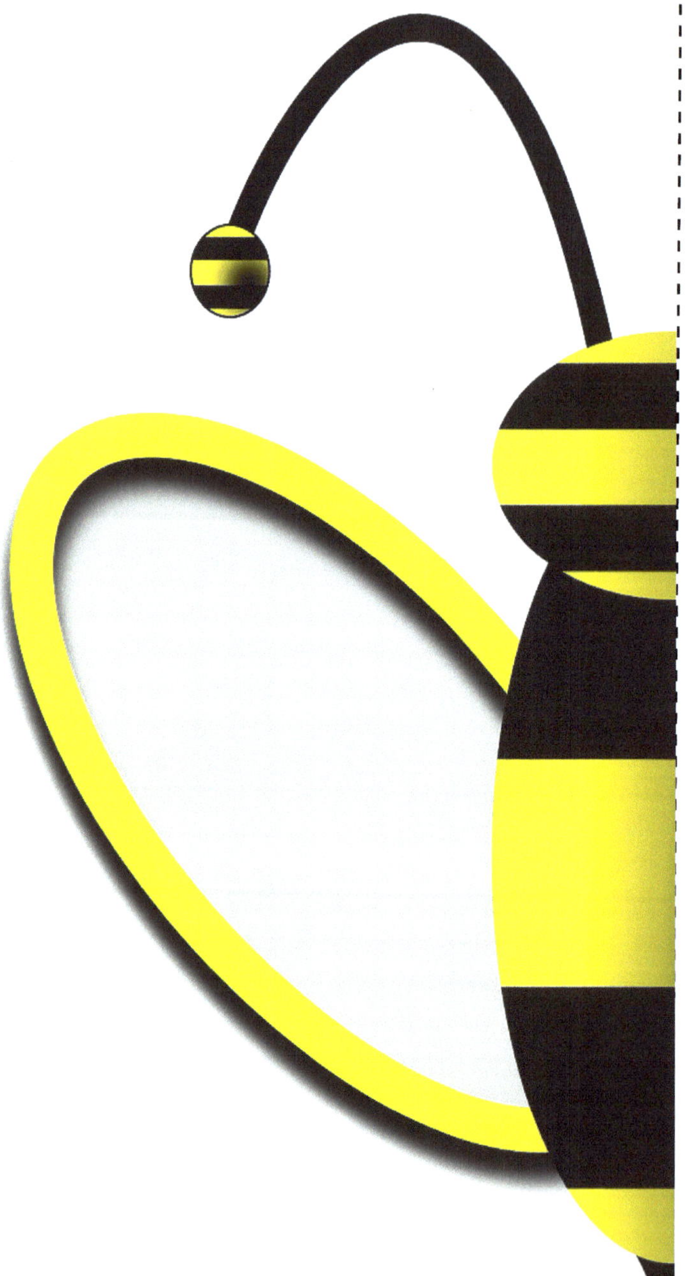

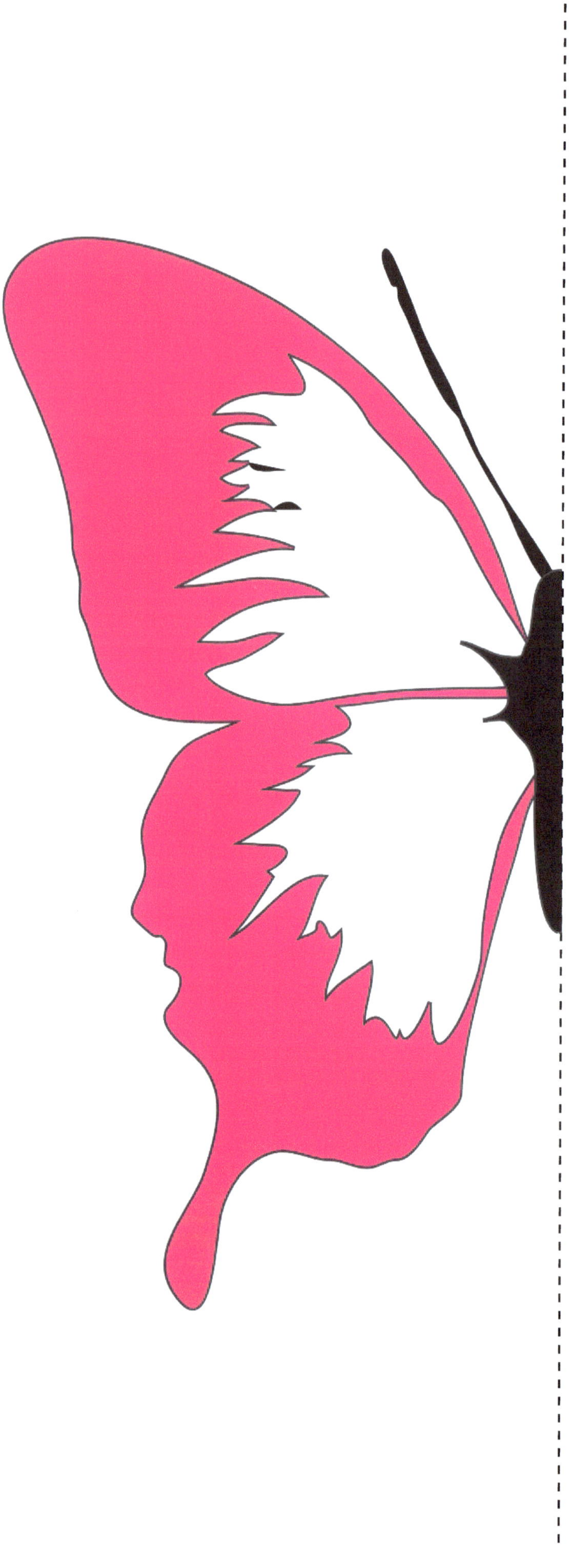

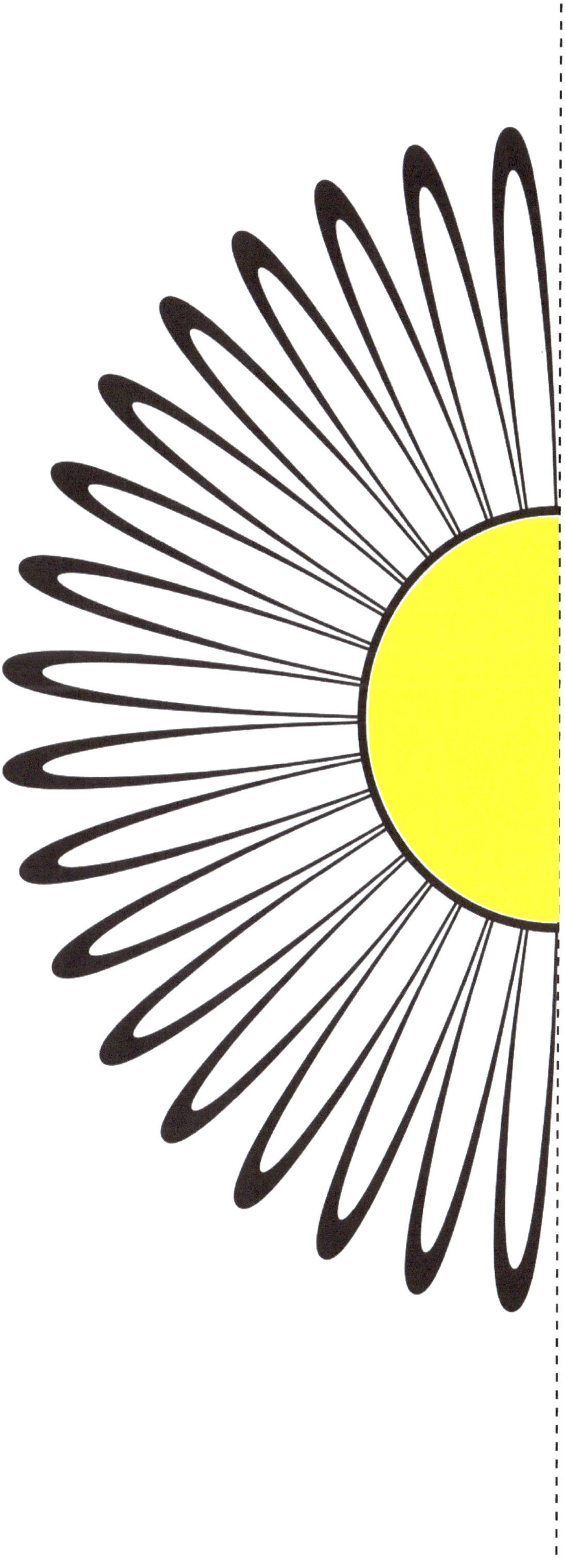

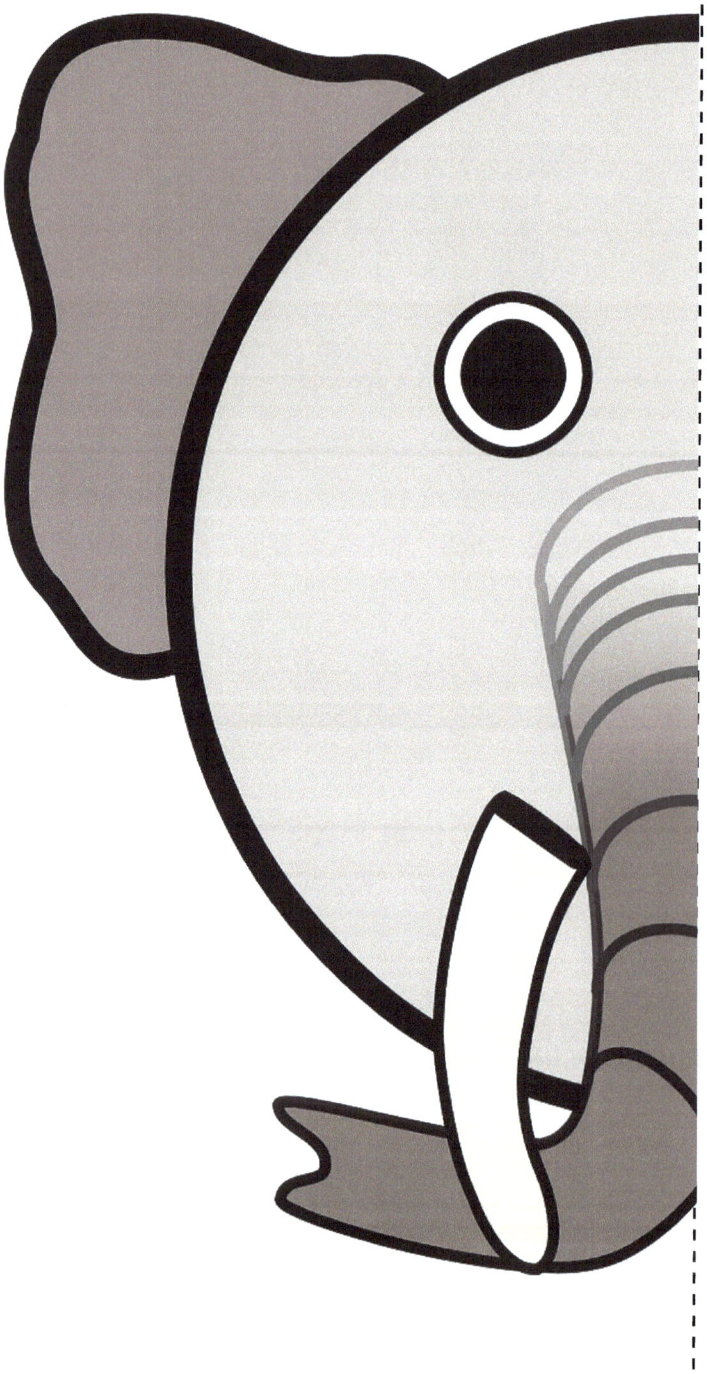

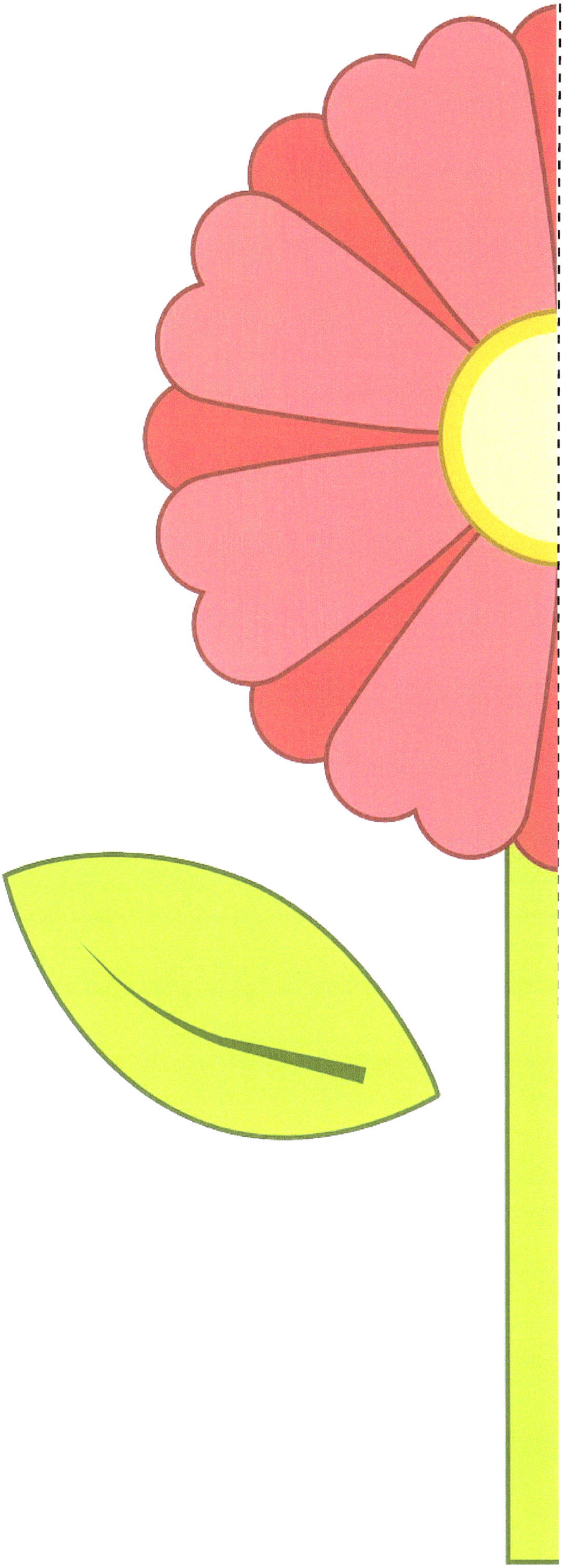

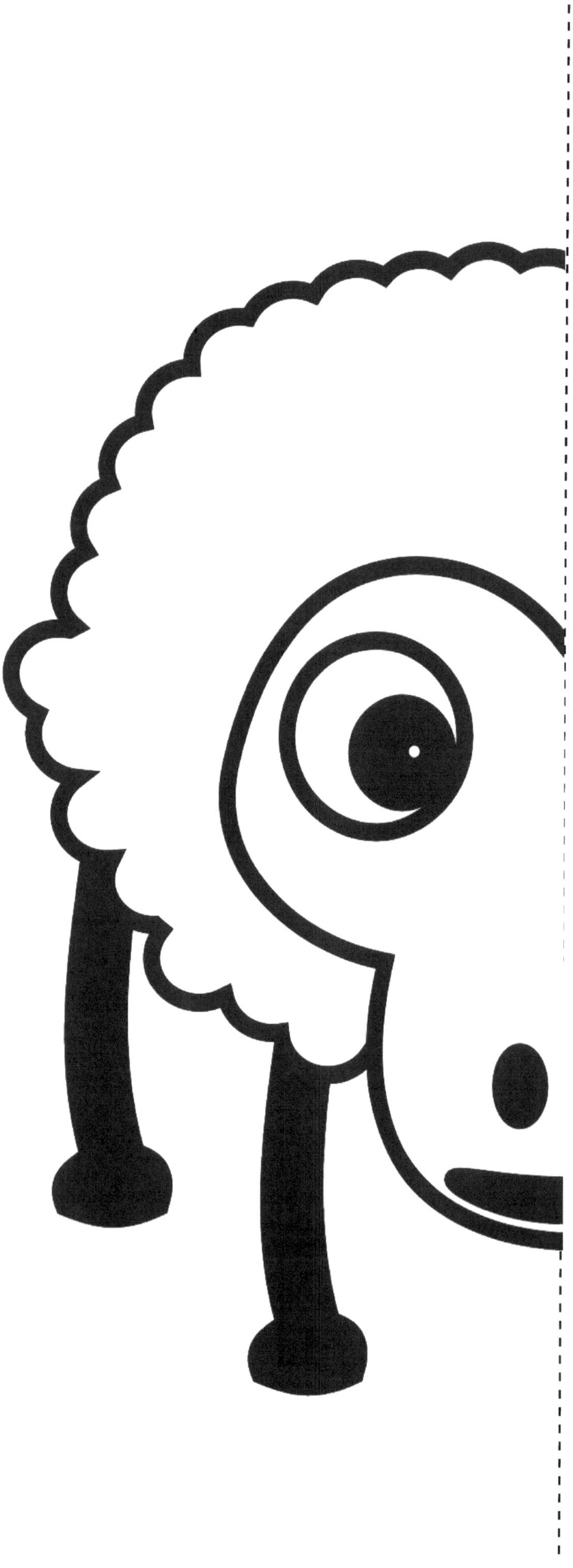

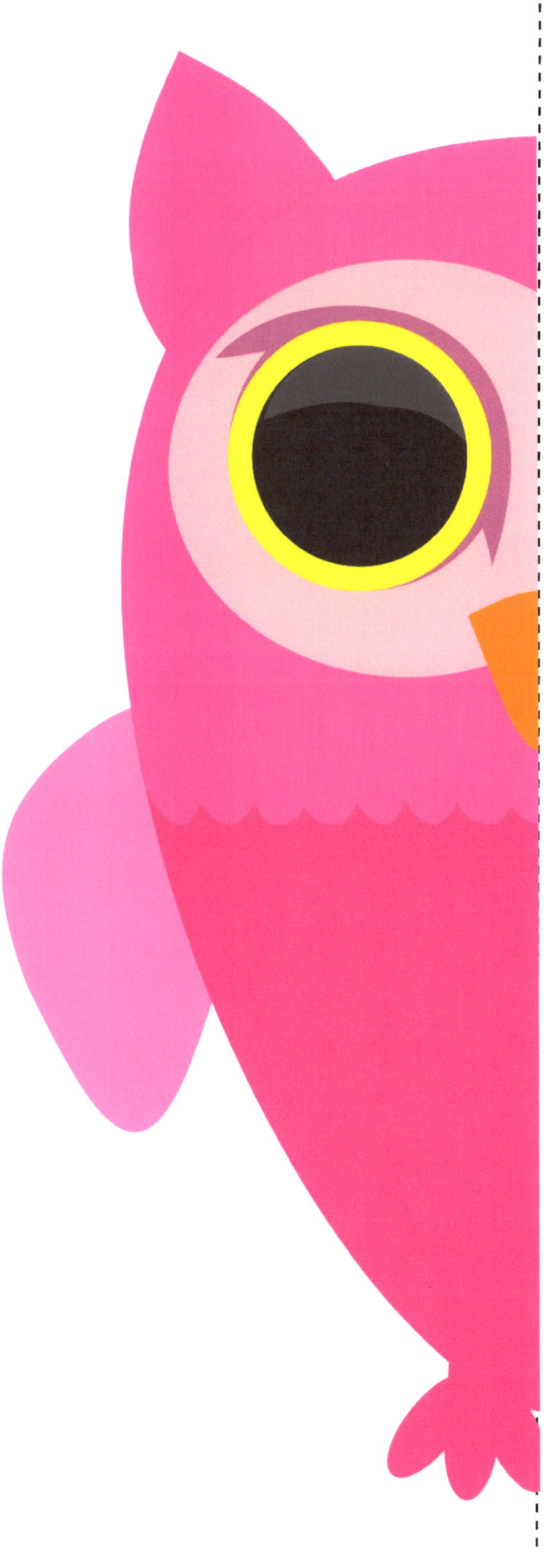

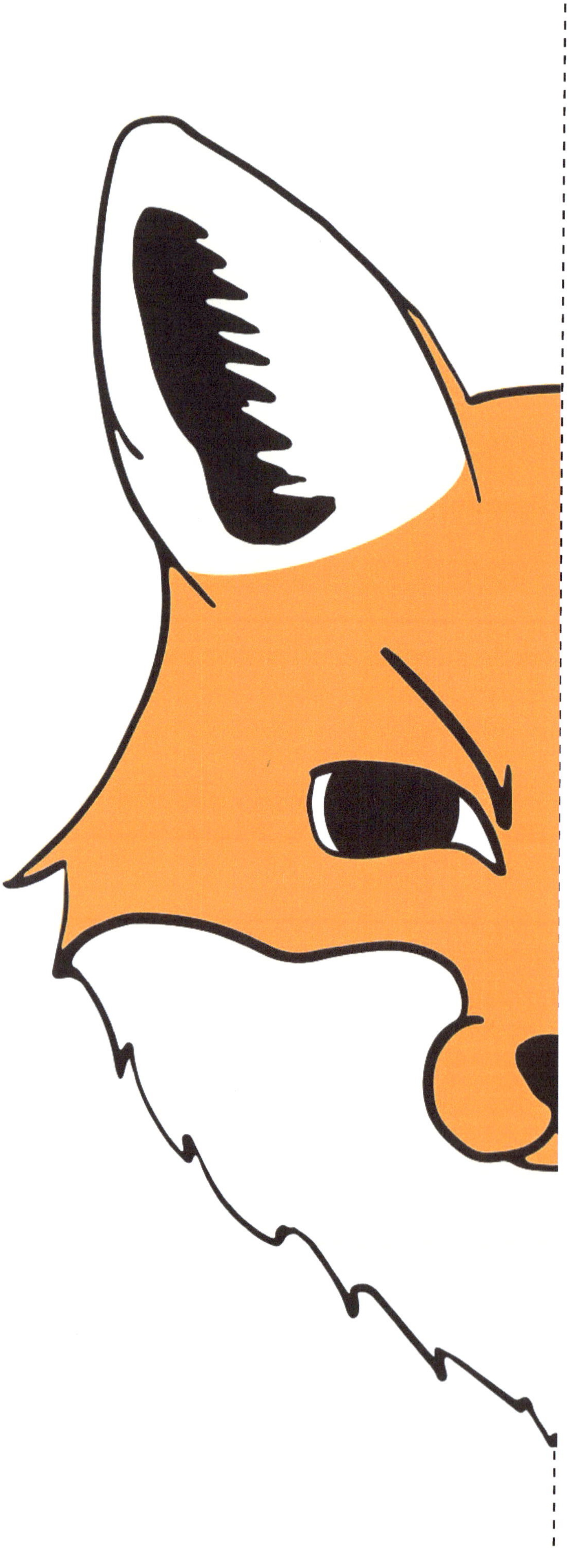

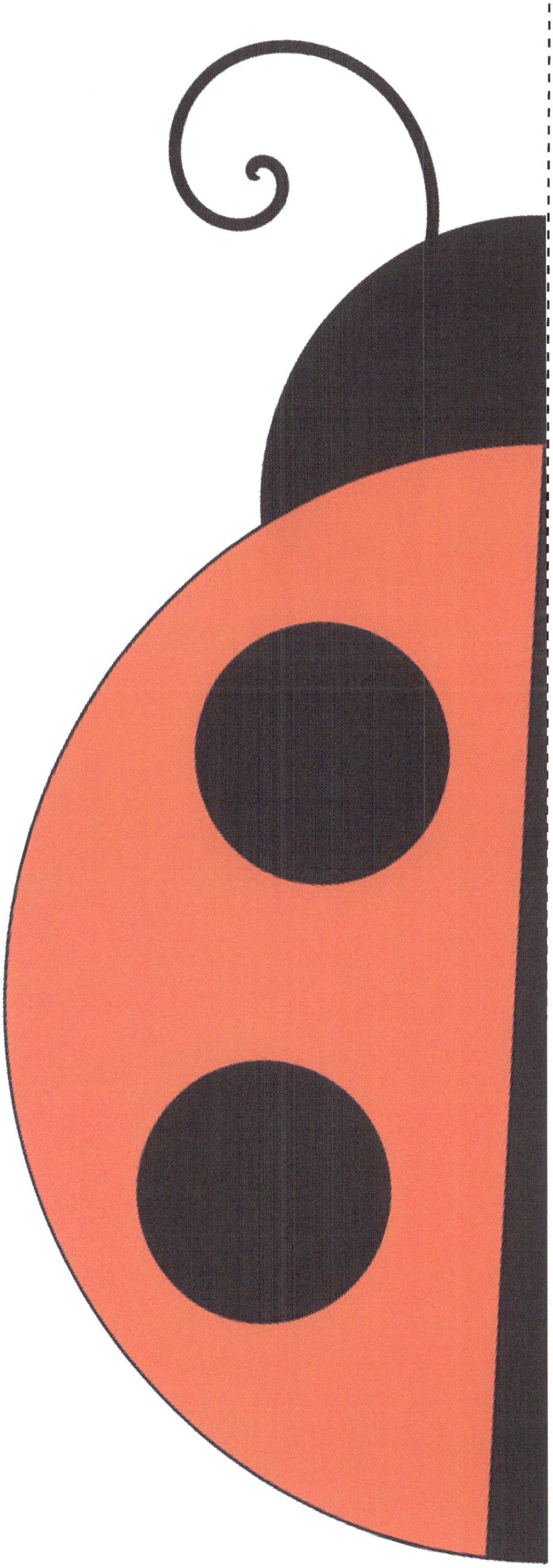

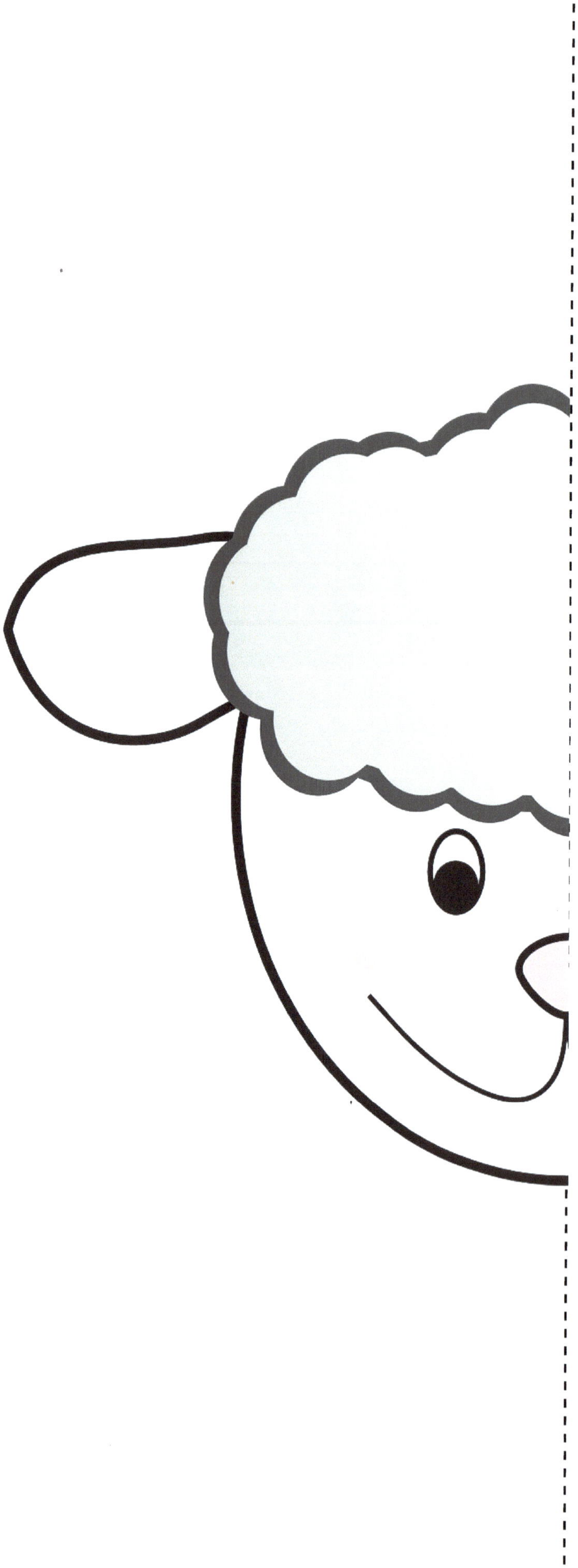

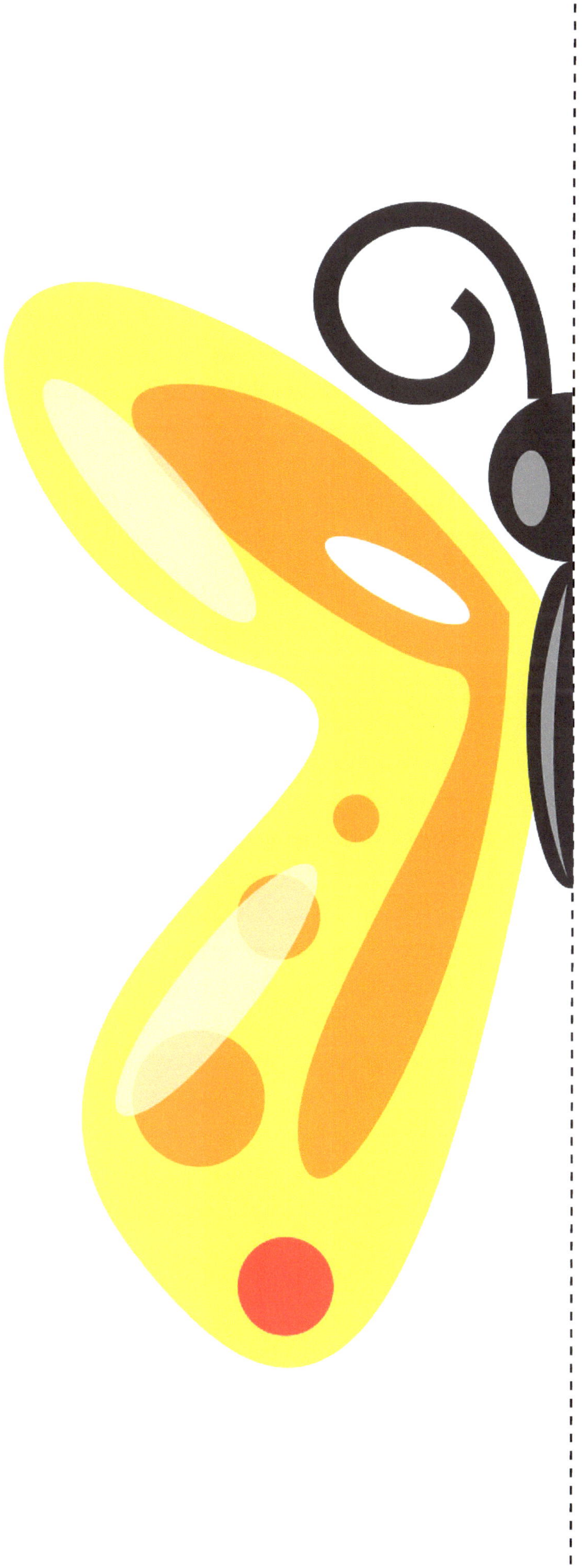

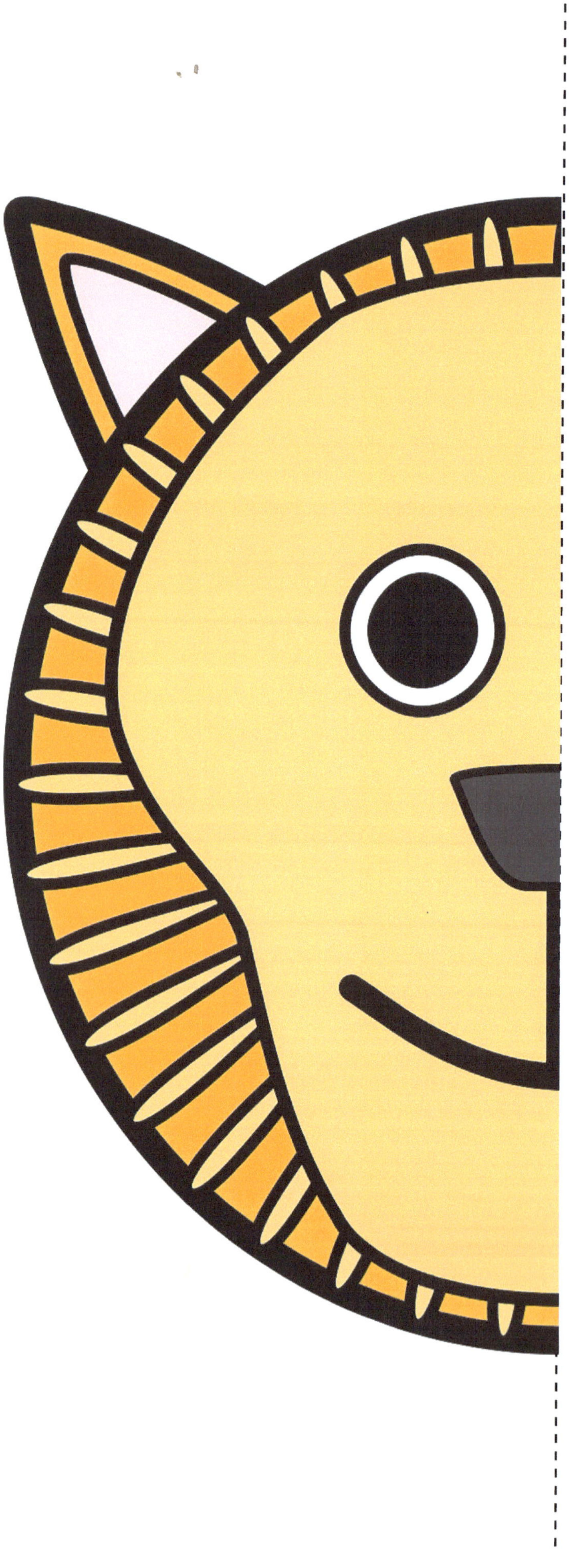

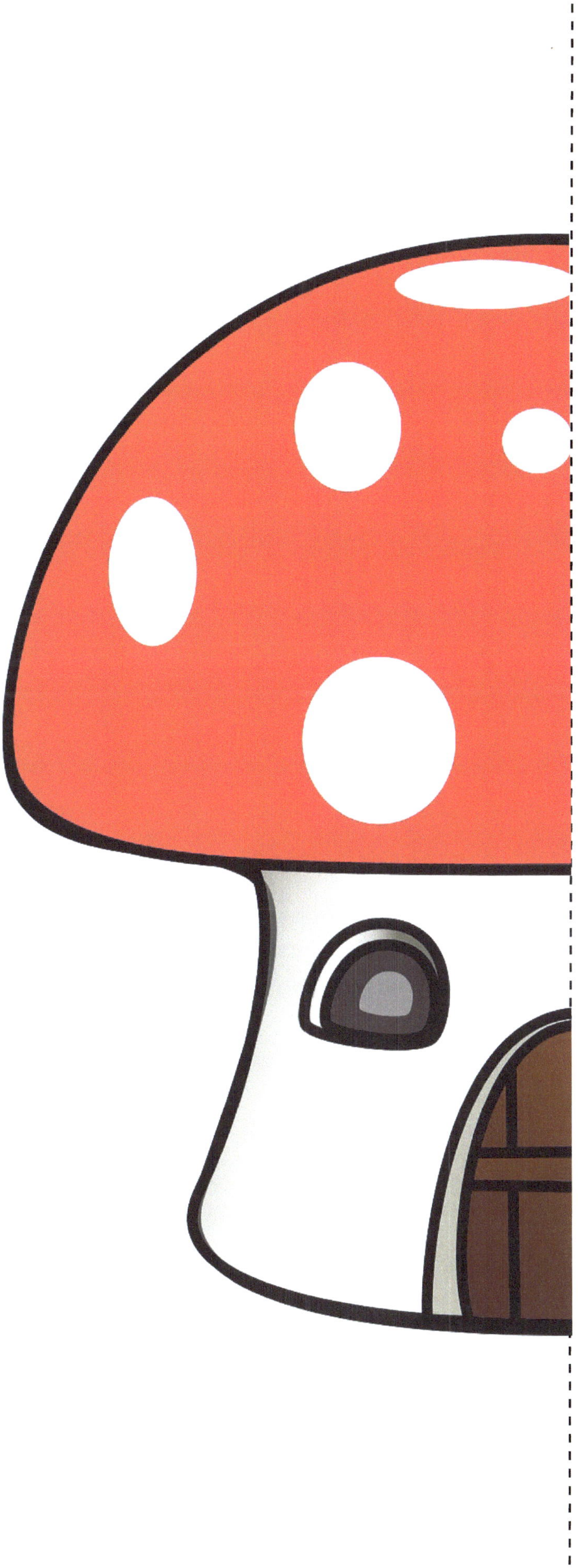

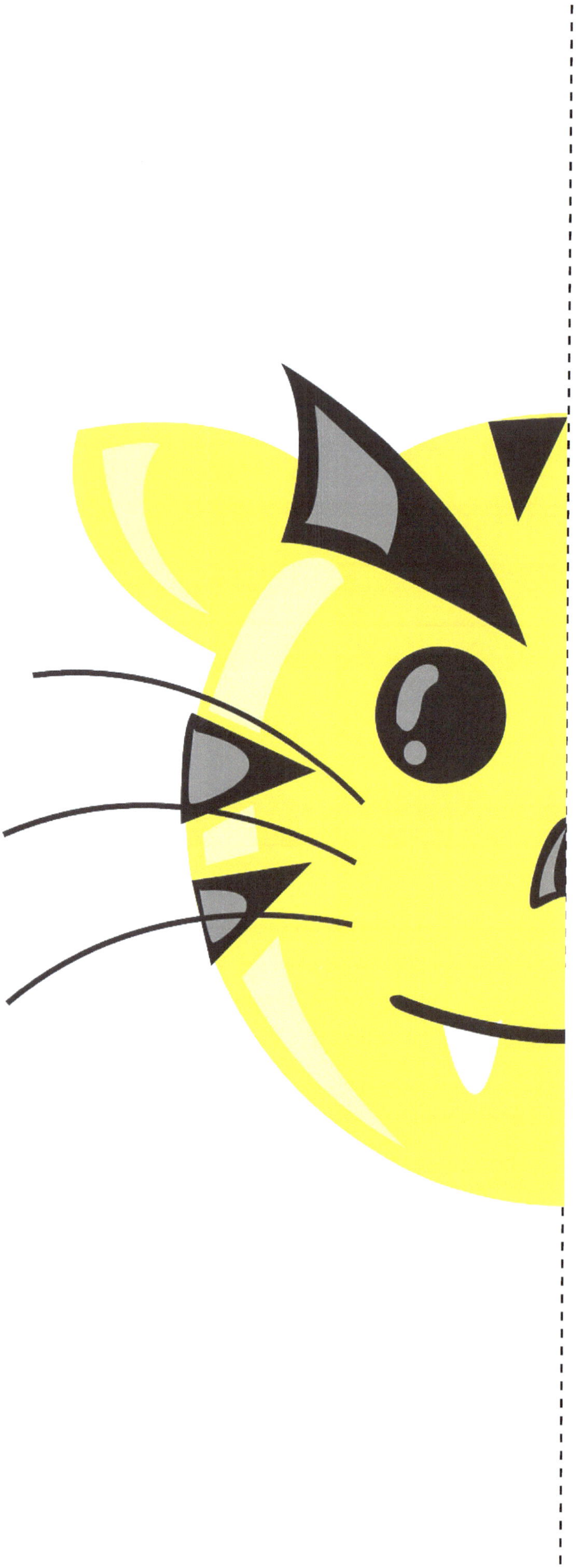

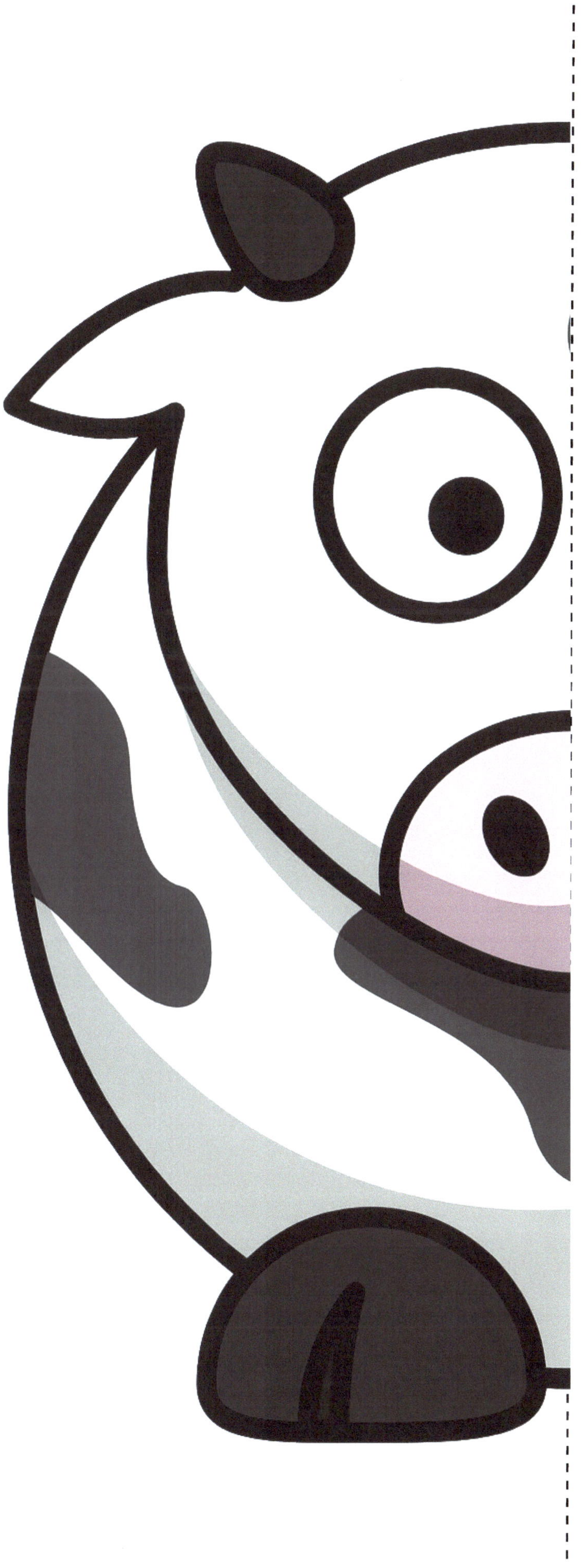

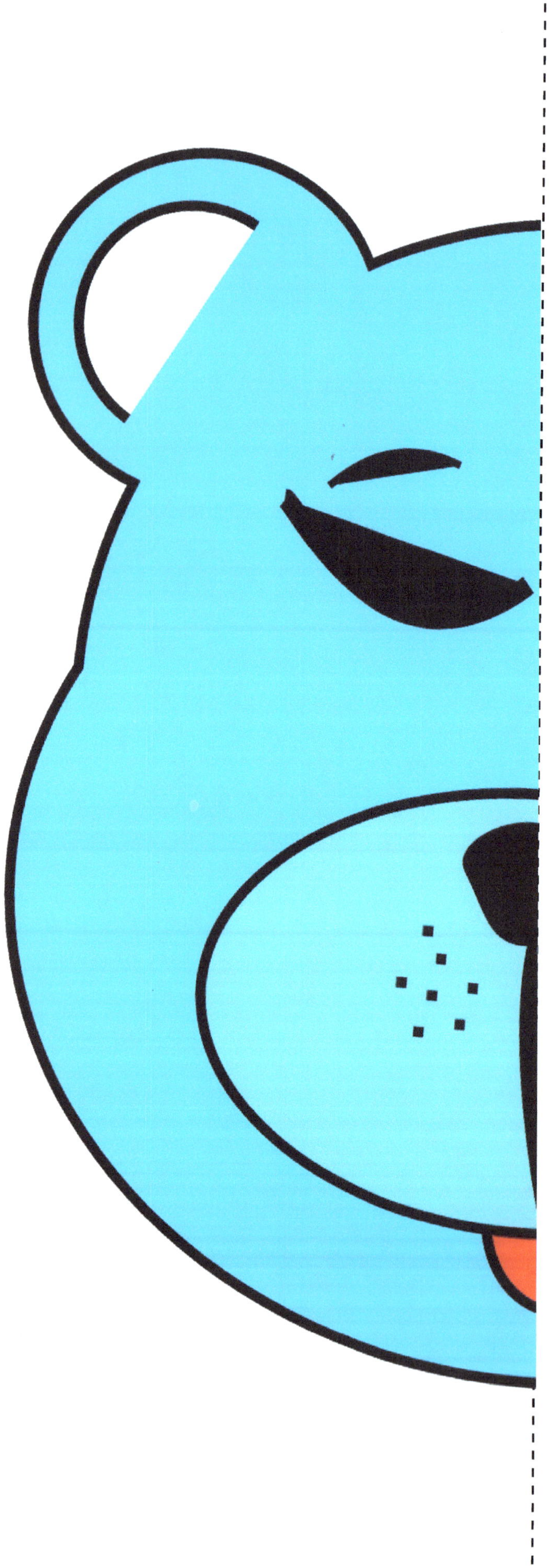

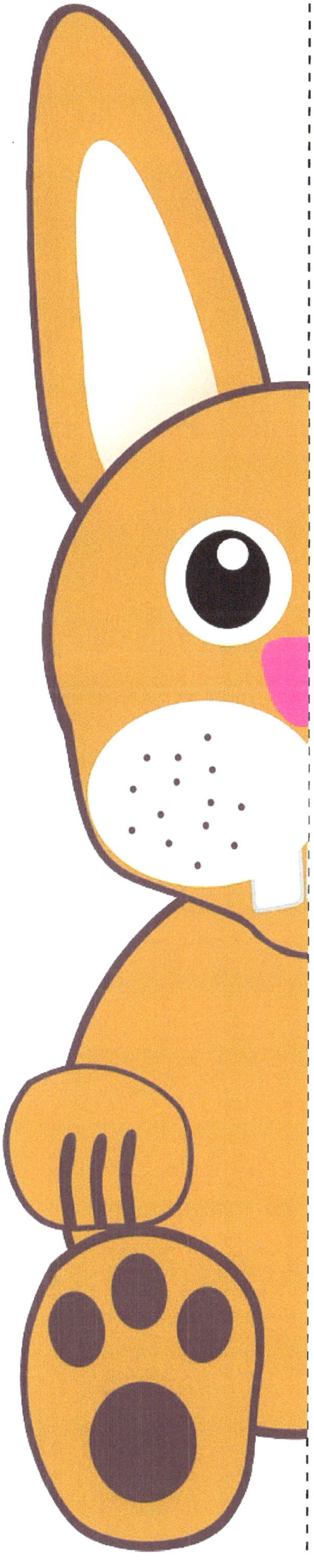

www.ingramcontent.com/pod-product-compliance
Lightning Source LLC
Chambersburg PA
CBHW051057180526
45172CB00002B/680
* 9 7 8 1 0 7 6 0 0 3 9 9 7 *